RECESSION LESSONS:

SELLING THROUGH ADVERSITY

TOM RAY

RECESSION LESSONS:

SELLING THROUGH ADVERSITY

Jim Doyle & Associates
7711 Holiday Drive
Sarasota, FL 34231
(941) 926-7355
tom@jimdoyle.com
www.jimdoyle.com
www.doyleondemand.com

This book is dedicated to the account executives, sales managers, and advertisers who allow me to offer help in the worst conditions we've ever seen, both then and now. And to my wife, Darlene, who is always by my side, in good times and in bad.

CONTENTS

THE SET UP

April 2, 2020

I had five Zoom video meetings today with five individual account executives from across the country. Emotions ranged from optimism to fear to helplessness to utter defeat. It's tough out there. Damn tough. For everyone.

We are in a very difficult but rewarding business. We help local businesses survive and thrive, we apply our advertising and marketing expertise, using the tools our companies provide—both over the air and digitally—and we help businesses educate and inform their target. It's all I've ever done for more than 35 years, and I love it.

Over the course of those 35 years, I've seen good times and some not-so-good times. When the economy is humming, when consumer confidence is high, when business is good, it's a blast. Optimistic business decision-makers are apt to try new and different things as the risk is lower. Mistakes hurt less. It's fun. When things are iffy, when disruption is in the air, when gas is $3 a gallon—then $4—when political uncertainty reigns, it gets a little more serious dealing with local decision-makers.

Then there are events that are watershed—specific turning points that change the game.

October 22, 1987. "Black Monday." The DJIA fell by 508 points (22.6%), the largest percentage drop in one day in history. I was selling radio advertising. I was young—in my late twenties. I knew something was serious, but I didn't quite understand the scope of it. All I knew was that my billing took a hit, for a while. Thankfully, I worked at a classic rock powerhouse, and I had enough bars and nightclubs on my list to get me through. (We like to drink when things go south).

It was the worst I'd ever seen.

September 11, 2001. 9/11. I was the Director of Sales for an Internet development company. We were in our weekly production meeting when our lead developer's wife called three times to tell him a plane had crashed into the tower. We went on with our meeting. We spent the rest of the day in the big conference room watching the news, in silence. I remember looking into the skies for days, at nothing. No planes. No white streaks. I think our spirits were more hurt than our business. It was a game-changer.

It was the worst I'd ever seen.

September 29, 2008. The Great Recession. On September 29, 2008, the stock market collapsed when the U.S. House of Representatives rejected a bailout bill. I was traveling the country as a sales and advertising consultant (as I still do). I had been feeling the effects of the failing economy all year. Throughout the course of 2008, I met ag-related businesses in the Midwest who were nervous about prices. I met car dealers all over the country who were watching inventory, I met furniture store owners, bankers, home builders, and people in every other category imaginable who were beyond nervous. By October 2008, every business I met with was in panic mode. So were the managers and account executives at the media outlets I teamed with.

It was the worst I'd ever seen.

And so, I spent the years of the Great Recession—starting really in 2007 all the way through to 2011 for many—meeting local advertisers across the United States. I travelled at least every other week, racking up frequent flier miles and visiting local businesses. I worked side by side with local media account executives and managers trying to save budgets, create ideas, stay positive, be realistic. But it was tough.

It's tough when you say to a business owner, "Thanks for your time today. I'll be back in three weeks and I'll bring you some ideas." And the business owner says, "Brother, I may not be in business in three weeks." That happened to me more than once.

It's tough when you hop into an account executive's car for our first ride of the week together and I enthusiastically greet them with, "Hi! How's it goin'?" And their response is, "Well, I'm gonna make twenty-grand less this year. How do you think it's goin'?" That happened to me more than once... a month.

The Great Recession. Nothing "Great" about it. It sucked. Businesses went under. Good people, good AE's, good managers left our business. Unlike the single event of 9/11, it was a slow burn. If 9/11 was a Mike Tyson first-round knockout punch, the Great Recession was an Ali-Frazier 15-round slobberknocker. You just didn't know when it was going to end!

Did I mention it was the worst I'd ever seen?

Until now.

March 11, 2020. The Coronavirus/COVID-19 Pandemic. On March 11, 2020, a player on the Utah Jazz preliminarily tested positive for COVID-19. It triggered a league-wide suspension of play. Things just got real. Sure, we had all been aware of this virus for months. In January of 2020, Jim Doyle & Associates hosted 150 high-performing managers at our Boot Camp. My kickoff introduction on Sunday morning, January 26th, was basically a 15-minute monologue of jokes. I had rehearsed the day before with my wife. "Welcome to the Suncoast of Florida! Home to some of the most beautiful beaches in the world. I hope you have a chance to visit them while you're here. But be careful, there have been reports of Coronavirus on Siesta Key Beach. Yeah. You get on the beach, see someone open a Corona, and you immediately want one!" Thankfully, my wife nixed that joke.

For me, the NBA season suspension was the moment the game changed. It was here, it was real. And it started the dominoes tumbling. Events cancelled. Leagues suspended play. My schedule fell apart. Jackson, MS on March 19th, postponed. Amarillo on the 26th, cancelled. Miami on March 31st, don't even think about it.

By Monday, March 16th, our team huddled on our regular Monday morning Zoom meeting and began strategizing. By Thursday the 19th, we were hosting a webinar for all of our media partners titled, "Dealing with Disruption." Attendance exceeded our 500-registrant capacity. We gave tips on how to Work from Home Effectively and Tips for Video Conferencing. By Tuesday, March 24th, I was a guest on the Kentucky State Broadcasters roundtable call in with Governor Andy Beshear and former US Senator and President of the NAB, Gordon Smith. By Friday, March 27th, I was hosting a Special Edition of our MONEY CALL, sharing an hour of ideas to take to advertisers to address COVID-19.

By the hour, we were learning of advertiser cancellations... massive, immediate cancellations... for our partners in markets big and small, all over the country. We were told not to show up at the office. On Tuesday, March 31st, I spent a half hour on Facebook Live, reading children's stories as a way to give our "work from home/teach from home/try to keep it together from home" parents a break. I ended my Facebook Live session by playing Bob Marley on my ukulele. "Don't worry, about a thing. Every little thing is gonna be all right."

This is the worst I've ever seen.

I'm not a "futurist." I don't like to predict things. I'm much more of a "present-ist" (I think I made that word up). I like to address what's happening today. So, I'll leave the prognostication to those much smarter than I, except to say, it's bad and it's going to be bad.

Today, while I was meeting with five different account executives, I thought, "What can I tell these wonderful AE's about selling through adversity?" I said, "Stay active. Action promotes activity." And "don't lose alone. Keep your managers in the loop on everything." That was a mantra at the radio station where I worked during the 80's. I wrote an article about it during the Recession. I said, "Avoid the naysayers. Focus on ROI. Reduce risk..." I wrote articles about all of this during the Recession.

I've written a lot for our various Jim Doyle & Associates newsletters, publications, and training platforms. In fact, in 2008, I committed to writing at least one article a week for our previously published AE newsletter, *The Achiever's Circle*. It was probably my most prolific period of regular writing. The content was driven by my every-other-week travels and the 25-plus meetings per week with local advertisers. Throughout 2008 and 2009, the conditions were the worst I'd ever seen, for advertisers and account executives.

This book is a collection of those articles. It's all the lessons I learned during my time on the streets leading up to, and in the midst of, the darkest days of the Great Recession and the recovery period thereafter. The articles are a collection of thoughts on sales, advertising, and inspiration/motivation. I'll share the articles as they were originally written, and I'll add some updated commentary. The lessons we learned from the last "worst I've ever seen," can help us navigate the dark waters ahead.

"Those that fail to learn from history, are doomed to repeat it." -Winston Churchill

"Fool me once, shame on you. Fool me... you can't get fooled again." -George W. Bush/Pete Townshend

SECTION 1:

SELLING THROUGH ADVERSITY

NOTES FROM THE PAST TWO WEEKS ON THE STREETS

ORIGINALLY PUBLISHED: 10/11/2008

2020 Perspective – Wow! I chose this as Chapter 1 of Recession Lessons because I originally wrote it on October 11th, 2008. It was the absolute lowest, darkest, ugliest time I'd ever seen. I felt the exact same emotions on March 12, 2020.

Some thoughts on the current conditions...

I just spent two weeks on the streets. I met with 50 different businesses across 4 markets. I don't have to tell you it's tough out there. Here are some thoughts on what's going on and what to do about it...

Consumers are paralyzed. "Want" purchases just aren't being made. From the cosmetic surgeon who said she hasn't had an inquiry in two weeks to the high-end furniture store whose traffic was nil, even the wealthy (or former wealthy!) are out of the game. Hence, your advertisers are paralyzed. Many have decided to pull back because they feel they can't force traffic.

What can you do about it? Stay close. Don't run and hide. You've probably taken a cancellation or two in the past couple of weeks—so be it. Stay on top of those who cancelled so you can be first in line when they decide to come back. Bring those clients regular feedback from your market and prove you have your finger on the pulse of what's happening locally.

It's okay to say, "I don't know." I had many clients ask me when I thought things would recover. One story, in particular, stands out. I was meeting with a very big fitness chain—20 facilities in multiple markets. The owner was distressed. Not only was he not signing any new members, but many of his current members were cancelling. He'd just finished saying that he had heard things wouldn't recover until 4th quarter '09. He asked what I thought. Here's what I said, "I don't know. Nobody knows. A year from now sounds like a safe guess, but I heard things should get better by 4th quarter '08 a year ago! Here's what I do know. At some point, things will begin to recover. Those who are prepared to take advantage of opportunity will win. My advice is to watch closely, look for openings, be guerrilla, and be smart." The client appreciated that I was honest.

Seriously, nobody really does know when things will recover. We can all offer an opinion, just like the pundits on CNN, but who cares. Rather than trying to predict the future, I'd steer the conversation toward opportunistic solutions. I told the fitness facility that first quarter will still represent 40% of his annual business and that he needs to be ready to take advantage of it. I also told him that in tough economic times, people turn to comfort foods like donuts and ice cream and that might bode well for him soon!

Who's advertising and who isn't?

Here's who was optimistic in the past two weeks...

- The Honda store that was having no problems with financing
- The community college that focuses on retraining back-to-schoolers (they refer to them as nontraditional students) who have lost their jobs
- The heavy discount retailers with words like "wholesale" and "salvage" in their names
- Credit unions are still lending

Here's who was in total fear...

10

- Every domestic auto dealer I met with
- Furniture and mattress stores
- Fitness centers ("it's the first thing to go and the last thing to come back in poor economic times")
- Cosmetic spas and cosmetic dentists
- Travel agencies
- Home builders and remodelers

Some things to do over the next few weeks...

- Always have success stories to share. Be prepared to tell a success or two. Do you know about a business that's weathering this economic storm favorably? Tell your clients. Get with your teammates and share those stories of good traffic days or successful sales. It will make your clients feel better to hear of other businesses that are still achieving some success.
- Offer opportunities. Call anyone who's on with you and sell them the cancellation inventory you may have. Those who are still on the air may want to take advantage of the "deal" inventory.
- Discuss plans for the recovery. Ask your clients what they intend to do when things settle. Then have a floating plan in place that they can initiate when ready. Talk about copy points, etc., so they can react faster.
- Focus on "need purchase" businesses, not "want purchase" businesses. Want purchases are put on hold for now—hot tubs, vacations, new snow mobiles are all on the back burner. Things like plumbers and HVAC guys are still in need when pipes burst or the heat won't come on.

As an old colleague of mine used to say, "In chaos, there is opportunity!"

CHAPTER 2

ACTION PROMOTES ACTIVITY

ORIGINALLY PUBLISHED: 10/11/2008

2020 Perspective – I wrote this article on the same day, 10/11/2008, as the article in Chapter 1. I wrote this one for our Leader's Edge Coaching Program for sales managers. I still believe action promotes activity. This year, I've committed to going for a run or walk every day at 4 pm when I'm not travelling. Inevitably, I return to the office with another idea to share—move.

I visited about 5 different car dealerships last week. I think they were actually happy to see media salespeople in the showroom—they were so lonely! This economic crisis and credit crunch have absolutely devastated their traffic.

One dealership showroom had a different feel from the rest, though. I met with the General Manager of a Nissan dealership in the South. The atmosphere of his showroom had a bit of a buzz to it. As we were discussing his business, he told me that in the past week he purchased a basketball hoop and had it installed in the back. He told me that he encouraged his sellers to throw the football around outside. His reasoning was that action promotes activity. He said that in light of current conditions, every up was critical and he didn't want his team "flat" when they had their opportunity. He said he liked the idea of his guys moving around and staying sharp in the downtime between ups.

He also knew that anyone walking into a dealership in

these times was a real prospect, so he was making sure his sellers were at their peak for each customer.

Think about his approach—action promotes activity. When all the other dealerships have commiserating car salespeople hanging around talking about how lousy things are, this guy has his team shooting hoops and throwing the football around to stay sharp.

What's going on with your team? Are they sitting at their desks searching CNN.com, reading story after story of dismal news? Are they grabbing coffee together and planning their next career?

The last couple of weeks can suck the life out of even the best of us. Are you doing your part to keep your team active? Here are some very simple suggestions you might want to try:

- Bring a ball to your next sales meeting and throw it to a team member. Have them answer an objection. Once they answer, they throw the ball to a different team member who then answers a different objection.
- Have each team member stand up in your sales meeting and deliver a brief success story. Follow each story with a round of applause.
- Take a random ice cream sandwich break (a la Michael Scott from The Office). Pick an afternoon that you're going to bring ice cream treats to the staff. Take fifteen minutes to gather everyone for a stand-up break.
- Put some toys around the sales area, a putting green, a Nerf basketball hoop or a dart board, things to lighten the mood. If you, as leader, take the initiative to encourage a fun and active atmosphere, the team will follow.

Take it upon yourself as manager to keep a watchful eye on your team. More than ever before, you need to show some special attention to those players who seem to be struggling more in these current conditions. When you sense the mood sinking, you have to step in.

If you've ever attended a live Tony Robbins seminar, you know that every 45 minutes or so, Tony has the entire audience get up, move around, even give shoulder rubs to each other. He understands that action promotes activity.

Will putting up a basketball hoop help the Nissan dealership sell 5 more cars this month? Maybe not, but it may make a difference in how sharp the salespeople are as they approach the next valuable up.

CHAPTER 3

STUCK IN PENDING HELL

ORIGINALLY PUBLISHED: 6/6/2009

<u>2020 Perspective</u> – Don't get comfortable with a "maybe." It may look good on projections, but it'll burn you down the road. Avoid Pending Hell, no matter what the year.

During our recent Call In Day, one Achiever's Circle member called to say that he was having trouble closing a bunch of proposals. He'd presented quite a few proposals, yet the clients were just sitting on them. They hadn't said "yes" yet, but they hadn't said "no" either.

This is what we call "Pending Hell." It's called Pending Hell because it can be a nightmare for an AE. You've got all this potential sitting out there, but nothing is closing, so it really amounts to a whole bunch of nada! Plus, you've included it on your projections to management, making you accountable for it.

For some AE's, Pending Hell can be a comfort zone. Because they haven't gotten "no's," they feel good about the amount of business out there. For Achievers, Pending Hell is no place to get comfortable! You want to constantly advance the sales process and being stuck in limbo does you no good.

Here are three tips to avoid Pending Hell...

1. **Always put expiration dates on your proposals.** You know that your business is fluid. Rates change, availability changes, political windows occur, etc. Don't put out a proposal that doesn't have a deadline for

15

decision. And, make it clear to the client during the presentation that the strategy (schedule, sponsorships, promotions, etc.) has a limited time of availability. Typically, a three-week window is enough time for a client to make a decision and a fair enough window for you to honor rates, promotions, etc.

Note: If you're presenting limited or first-come opportunities, make sure that's clearly noted in the proposal. Fear of loss is a powerful motivator.

2. **"What would it take to get you to move forward today?"** Get yourself out of Pending Hell by asking the direct question, "What would it take?" By posing this very direct question, you'll learn where you stand in relation to a close. A client may respond by saying, "Really, there's nothing you can do to get me to agree today." Well, at that point you know that you're much closer to a "no" than a "yes," and you can react accordingly. Sometimes, you'll get an answer that you can work with to enable a close. "You'd have to include a news sponsorship." Or, "free production" might be an answer that means you're closer to a close. Of course, some clients will answer with things that are out of your control, like, "Guarantee the recession to be over!" In this case, I'd re-phrase the question and ask again, "Of the things I can control, what would it take to get you to move forward today?"

Note: Be prepared with things to offer to help the client along with their answer. Many clients won't know (or won't say) what it would take to get them to say yes today, so be prepared with suggestions. "If I could include a news sponsorship, would that help you decide today?"

3. **Pull the plug.** Get yourself out of Pending Hell by pulling the plug on the proposal. If a client is sitting

on your presentation and won't give you a definitive "yes" or "no," just pull the plug on it. The smartest way to pull the plug is to offer something else. Represent with a different idea, whether it be in creative or strategy. The message you're sending says, "Well, obviously you didn't love what I brought you last time, so I'm taking it off the table and replacing it with a different idea." If the client really did like the proposal, they won't let you take it away, or they'll ask for the parts they liked, and you now have better information with which to work.

Don't be comfortable in Pending Hell. It's a nightmare for you and your manager. Your goal is to be constantly advancing the sale, so you have to take action when things have stalled. Use these techniques to get you out of Pending Hell or avoid it altogether.

CHAPTER 4

"ALL OUR ADVERTISING HAS BEEN PUT ON HOLD"

ORIGINALLY PUBLISHED: 4/7/2009

2020 Perspective – I'm sure you're hearing it. "We're not doing anything right now." "Everything has been put on hold." For these, I like the response, "Is that a NO for now, or a NO forever?" Do something for your client during the downtime, so that when the time comes for them to be active again, you are thought of first.

Your regular client has said, "All our advertising has been put on hold." They've been with you for a long time, but now, under current conditions, they've had to pull back. Sound familiar? Understand that this is now an opportunity... **for your competition**!

Here's what I mean...

Recently, I was in a market and we had a presentation appointment scheduled with a new client. The client had been prospected off one of the competing stations in town. Just before our meeting, the AE said to me, "When I called to confirm, she said she'd be happy to meet, but that they've recently put all media on hold for now."

"Fantastic!" I said. The AE looked at me and said, "Why is that fantastic?"

I said, "She'd been on your competition regularly before, right? She was tough to even get in front of for a Time Out Call, right? Well, now we don't have to worry about your competition because she's not on them anymore due to the hiatus."

"All our advertising has been put on hold," means everyone in the market is starting from the same point moving forward. She wouldn't have put any outlet on hold that had been delivering measurable results. What she has clearly said is, "I don't think the other guys have been delivering measurable results."

All we have to do is go in and prove that we can deliver measurable results, and now it's easier to replace the incumbent station because she's not using them anymore.

The lesson here is that even when your clients are forced to go dark, for whatever reason, you need to keep a close relationship because your competition is out there working harder than ever to get in front of your loyal clients (just as you're working harder than ever to get in with their loyal clients). The natural tendency is to back off when the client says they're going on hold. This leaves you very vulnerable.

So, what *should* you do when the client goes on hold?
- Continue to be a resource: bring articles, category and market information
- Use the down time to do a full Time Out Call. As soon as you get the "going on hold" call, ask for a Time Out appointment.
- Do something extra for the client. What kind of impression would it make if you offered billboards or an online presence during the downtime?
- Look for valid reasons to end the hiatus and bring results-oriented ideas.

Remember, your competition is being very aggressive right now. Don't give them an opportunity to sneak into your regular clients during a hiatus.

CHAPTER 5

THE POWER OF A DEADLINE!

ORIGINALLY PUBLISHED: 11/20/2012

2020 Perspective – Never let a proposal go out the door without an expiration date!

I was reviewing an ad for a pizzeria recently. It was an okay ad, not fantastic. It talked about the great product (don't they all claim the BEST product) and it had an offer—$9.99 large pizza. I don't know what pizza sells for in your market, but to me, $9.99 for a large pepperoni pizza just sounded okay, it didn't sound like an astonishing offer.

Here's the big problem I had with the ad—there was no deadline! With no deadline, the offer sounded lame. It gave me the sense that $9.99 was the everyday price. The copy didn't even say, "for a limited time only!" It actually said, "…and now get a large pizza for $9.99…" There was no sense of urgency, no parameters or boundaries to the offer to give me the feeling that this was a special price. Just "now," and seemingly, for however long our ad budget lasts you'll "get a pizza for $9.99."

In the restaurant category, they call them LTO's—Limited Time Offers. I once had an owner of a national sandwich franchise tell me it didn't matter what the product was, if they said it was available for a limited time only, they'd sell a ton of product.

To me, this scenario demonstrates the power of a deadline.

Deadlines do several things…

First, a deadline creates urgency. A deadline can take a prospect from a "maybe, sometime soon" buyer to an action-taking prospect. There has to be some fear of loss and a deadline helps create that.

Second, a deadline helps determine ROI. A deadline can offer the advertiser a better opportunity to measure results. It's much easier to know whether a campaign worked when there's a specific offer with a deadline, as opposed to a branding campaign or a weak offer that has no expiration.

Finally, a deadline forces a buying decision. Will I make this purchase by this time? Without a deadline, the consumer isn't forced into making a yes/no decision because doing nothing (and not losing) is still an option.

So, if your clients are looking for measurable results from their advertising, don't miss this important ingredient. Have a deadline in place to force action.

Now, take that same concept and apply it to your proposals! Make sure your proposals have a deadline in the form of an expiration date. An expiration date on your proposal creates urgency and forces your client/prospect to make a buying decision, and most importantly, eliminates the "wait on it, do nothing" option.

CHAPTER 6

5 WAYS TO APPROACH DORMANT AND ORPHAN ACCOUNTS

ORIGINALLY PUBLISHED: 6/1/2010

2020 Perspective – At the earliest signs of improvement, get in front of those dormants and orphans with a valid business reason and an astonishing offer! In fact, today I received a phone call, an email message, and a LinkedIn message from a software company I had a demo with two years ago. I politely declined the salesperson's offer to re-connect, but I did commend him on working old leads during this Shelter in Place/Work from Home environment. He engaged me with a question or two, and guess what... I'll be re-visiting that software next week!

From Recession to Recovery, that's what I'm feeling out there. So here's something to consider—it's probably a good time to call on those dormant accounts. It is worth your while to get back in front of

- those former clients who cut you off last year
- prospects other reps called on and gave up on
- orphan accounts/prospects that no longer have a rep at your station

As things inch back towards normal, revisiting those opportunities from the past makes sense. But, just going back and saying, "Hey, are ya ready now?" isn't going to cut it. You need a strategy to approach dormant and orphan accounts because if they were already believers in your product, they wouldn't be dormant!

Here are some things to consider...

Ask the right questions. Start off by finding out why they went dormant. Ask them what you could do better, how you could adjust your offerings, how you might better meet their needs, etc. Take the feedback seriously and make adjustments where possible. Then, let them know that their feedback was heard and implemented.

Win them back with success stories. You've heard it from us a hundred times, "Facts tell, but stories SELL." You're not going to win back a client with more one sheets and ratings information. You will create interest with detailed stories of other like clients who are earning results with you.

Be persistent. They're probably not going to come back after one return visit by you. It will take a persistent and passionate approach, probably using a combination of face-to-face visits, emails and snail mail.

Identify what went wrong, admit to mistakes, and have a solution. If you lost a client, it was most likely because they felt your program didn't work. Figure out what went wrong and address it. Maybe you didn't have a compelling offer (or any offer at all!). Maybe your schedule wasn't targeted well or was too spread out. If they're not currently advertising with you, what does it hurt to go back and say, "Maybe we did it wrong. Maybe we should have had a stronger offer. I have way too many clients like you who are getting great results to give up on our partnership. I have an idea on how we could correct this..."

Provide an incentive. And make it an astonishing offer! A light whisper in the ear isn't going to wake up a sleeping client. You need to shout out loud with an astonishing offer. Think about your own buying habits. For whom are you a dormant account? Did you let a health club membership lapse or not renew a landscaping service? Have you ever stopped using a service or buying a product because you questioned its value? What would they have to do to get you back? Probably something pretty astonishing, right? You need to do the same with those dormant and orphan clients that have stopped using you.

CHAPTER 7

ANSWER A DIRECT QUESTION WITH A DIRECT ANSWER

ORIGINALLY PUBLISHED: 1/31/2010

2020 Perspective – I love the line from the great Roy Williams, the Wizard of Ads, who says, "When someone asks, 'How much?' the next word out of your mouth better be a number!"

I squirm in my seat every time I'm with a salesperson who can't answer a direct question from a client with a direct answer. Sometimes, folks, it's as simple as "yes" or "no."

I'm reminded of the Will Ferrell skit on *Saturday Night Live* when he's portraying Cubs announcer Harry Carey. He's interviewing a scientist played by Jeff Goldblum. He asks Goldblum, "If the moon were a piece of cheese, would ya eat it?" Goldblum, completely baffled, flounders for an answer. Ferrell's Harry Carey scolds, "It's an easy question, a simple yes or no will do. Answer, and let's move on!"

When a client asks, "How much is a spot in your 6 o'clock news?" he's not looking for a long answer. It's as simple as, "$850 per :30." The more we go into explanations of ratings, demand, packages and other complications, the less professional we look and the less trust we're developing.

I believe in this message so much that I've included it in my AE training sessions.

Last week, I held a training session with a sales staff in the Midwest. My power point slide with a picture of Will Ferrell portraying Harry Carrey popped on the screen and I delivered my "answer a direct question with a direct answer!" message. Later that evening, one of the AE's took me to meet with a car dealer with whom she'd been struggling. We had a full presentation and asked for a substantial UPGRADE amount.

The dealership owner was showing great signs of interest, but it was obvious we were pushing his comfort level on the budget.

"How much are these news spots?" he asked.

Without blinking, the AE replied, "$75 for the morning, $200 for the 6pm, $275 for the 11pm."

At that point the client got out his calculator and started massaging the schedule. We sat quietly as he scribbled a revised schedule.

"Okay, let's take out the access programming, heavy up in the morning news, and let's sell some cars..." he concluded!

We walked out with an agreement for just slightly less than what we were asking. The AE turned to me and said, "Thank goodness for your training today. I never would have just given him the rates had you not told us to answer a direct question with a direct answer."

Most AE's wouldn't have just given the rates. Most AE's would have gone into some long-winded, confusing answer about ratings, demand, time-of-the-month, day-of-the-week mumbo jumbo, which would have reduced their credibility and stalled the sale.

"How much are these?" is a pretty good buying sign in any situation, whether you're buying candy or commercials! When someone asks, tell them! And always answer a direct question with a direct answer.

CHAPTER 8

EMPATHY SELLING

ORIGINALLY PUBLISHED: 8/25/2008

2020 Perspective – I've adopted the phrase "tone deaf" a lot lately. I'm referring most often to our creative messages, but tone deaf also applies to how we're dealing with our clients and prospects. Show empathy. The "worst I've ever seen" is not only your worst, but theirs as well.

Let's start with a story. It's late afternoon on Friday and 40 people are waiting in the airport to board our 4 PM flight. At 4:20 PM, the airline announces that the fight has been delayed. Ya think?! At 4:30 PM, the gate agent tells everyone who has a tight connection that they can go back to the ticket desk to make alternate plans. Everyone is worried about making their connecting flight, irritated that the airline is offering little help, and downright frustrated at the notion of not getting home for the night. At 4:50 PM, we board for our hub city destination. As the 40 of us scurry to our seats so we can get moving, a bubbly flight attendant grabs the microphone and brightly welcomes us aboard. With no mention or apology for the late start, she cheerily runs through her announcements, seemingly oblivious to the fact that she's in front of a fairly hostile crowd.

I make a mental note: we must have empathy in selling, especially in today's challenging environment.

The flight attendant was doing her job, and under any other circumstances, doing it well—with enthusiasm and a smile. What she failed to recognize was the state of mind of her audience, her clientele if you will. A plane full of irritated passengers needed a little less "cheer" and a lot more sensitivity from her. As I was looking at spending the night in some city I didn't want to be in, missing my family for one more night, she was joking with airport employees. By the sound of the grumblings around me, I wasn't the only one feeling a little hostility brewing inside.

Had the flight attendant had any empathy, she would have been much more serious in her tone and reassured us that everything was being done to move us along as quickly and safely as possible.

"Empathy is about understanding the pain that the customer experiences, so that the aspirin can be tailored to their needs," says sales expert David Oliver. It's about being able to put yourself in the shoes of your client to really understand what they're feeling.

In today's challenging environment, our clients are very edgy. Most are facing a down year and they're not happy about it. At the point of being upset with a bubbly flight attendant who didn't sense my pain, I wondered if our clients might feel the same way with us if we don't handle them properly. I'm all about passion, enthusiasm and energy, but I wonder if that could ever backfire if I neglect to show empathy for a client's situation.

I hope that most of us are empathetic towards our clients. It's a fine line that we have to walk these days. We can't ignore the difficult conditions and we don't want to show defeat either.

What's the quickest way to gain an empathetic relationship with your clients? Through stronger diagnosis. This is a critical time to be performing those in-depth Time Out Calls. The more information you can uncover—the deeper you can dig—the more empathetic you can be to your client's needs.

- See like the customer
- Feel like the customer
- Think like the customer
- Use the words that come from the customer's heart

As I waited in line with the other passengers who missed connecting flights, I watched an angry passenger share his frustration with a customer service rep (that title was an oxymoron!). She looked up from her keyboard and simply said, "It's not my fault."

How about a heaping cup of empathy over here!

CHAPTER 9

THE 10 COMMON PROPOSAL MISTAKES

ORIGINALLY PUBLISHED: 3/28/2010

2020 Perspective – The biggest evolution in our proposal template over the past 10 years is brevity. We are really focused on keeping direct and to the point. We recommend that you make every slide re-audition for each customized proposal. If it's not absolutely critical to the overall success of the proposal, leave it out!

I've been reviewing lots of proposals lately and I've noticed some fairly common mistakes being made. Here are the top mistakes I see consistently being made...

1. Bad Titles. Most AE's think that the title isn't a very important step in the proposal-writing process, when in fact, it's a critical step. The title should make the proposal recipient want to jump in to see what you've put together for them! The title is not what you, the AE, think the client needs; it's a direct reflection of what the client told you they want solved. So, a title like, "Branding Family Smiles Dental" is a title an AE thinks makes sense. But is that really what the client wants? Do they want to brand their practice? Not really. What they really want is 30 new patients per month. So, a better title would be, "How to Achieve 30 New Patients Per Month." That's a proposal the client wants to jump into!

2. Thin Current Situations. After reviewing about twenty proposals recently, it seems as though most AE's are comfortable with a Current Situation of 4 or 5 bullet points. I say, put a little meat on them bones! Make sure you capture the meat of what's happening in the client's business, and somewhere in there should be some pain. If there's no pain (or growth opportunity), what do they need you for? The Current Situation doesn't reflect the *advertising* Current Situation. It's supposed to reflect the *business* Current Situation. The Current Situation should tell me a story, a vivid story.

3. No Success Stories. This may be the most powerful thing you could include in your proposals, especially in challenging conditions, yet many of us never include them. We say that selling is a system of reducing risk in the mind of the client. There's no better way to reduce risk than sharing powerful success stories. Most AE's would never think of presenting a proposal without their "We're #1" one sheets. Yet, from the client's perspective, those are far less convincing than a good story about a local business you've helped.

4. Weak Strategies. The extent of many "strategies" is that you should run ads so people hear about your business. That's it. Our proposal template calls it a Recommended Strategy. This is our opportunity to put the pieces of the marketing puzzle together and recommend a solution. This is the meat and potatoes of how you intend to fulfill your title promise. The Recommended Strategy should align with what you uncovered and included in the Current Situation.

5. Lack of Creative. Most of the proposals I review offer little in the way of creative execution. If there's any creative direction at all, it usually stops at a slogan or simple positioning statement (which many times is not specific enough to drive a result). I think every proposal should include a script. I know it's a lot of work, but that's what the client is really buying—their business offering brought to life. Include a script and the business owner can see their commercial in their mind's eye. Once they see it in their head, and if they really like it, budget limitations become less of an issue, the strength of your station becomes less of an issue, in fact, most other objections start to disappear. I've always said, "A hot idea melts a cold objection every time." You can miss on 90% of your proposal, but if you have the right creative, you're still in the game.

6. No "Recommended Strategy." Your proposal represents a solution to a problem. Your clients have some sort of pain that they want to correct through advertising. The Recommended Strategy page in your proposal is your opportunity to present your solution/strategy in a way that makes it understandable, rational, and in the best-case scenario, irrefutable. The mistake many AE's make is they completely skip this opportunity! Their proposals seem to go from "you have a problem" to "you should advertise," with no strategy or rationale as to how or why.

It's like asking a football coach, "What's your strategy for the big game on Sunday?" and he answers, "To score more points than the other team." That's not a strategy, that's a wish. A strategy would be, "Well, since their nose tackle got injured in the last game, we think they'll be soft against the run, so we're gonna pound the ball up the gut which should allow us to try some things deep every once in a while..." It's the X's and O's that are the strategy. A good proposal offers the X's and O's that lead to a victory.

7. TMI! Most proposals contain too much information. AE's insist on including every "one page" in their arsenal, oftentimes addressing things that don't need to be addressed. I recently reviewed a client presentation that had two anti-cable slides. I asked the AE, "Did the client say they were interested in cable?" The AE said, "No, I just wanted to include it, just in case..." I told the AE to take out those slides. If the client didn't bring it up as an issue, don't address it!

8. No Action Steps. The Action Steps slide we recommend is a power closing tool. The slide says:

Action Steps:

Proceed

Proceed with Changes

Stop the Process

It then offers a timeline of events, like copy approval, production completed, launch breakfast, etc.

This comes at the end of the proposal and the AE needs to simply say, "Now you have three choices in moving forward. If we nailed it, you can proceed, if we need to tweak something, we can proceed with changes, or if we completely missed the ball, we stop the process... what would you like to do?"

It's closing made easy! The client almost never says Stop the Process, so you're usually moving forward in some way.

9. No Signature Page. You have one goal when you make a presentation, to close the business. I am amazed how many AE's don't include a signature page so a client can approve the proposal. I know some stations "don't do business that way", but business, on all levels, is done with signatures and approvals, and a signature page let's your prospect know you want them to sign off on the presentation.

10. No Expiration Date. You should be including an expiration date on your proposals. You know that your business is fluid. Rates change, availability changes, political windows occur, etc. Don't put out a proposal that doesn't have a deadline for decision. And, make it clear to the client during the presentation that the strategy (schedule, sponsorships, promotions, etc.) has a limited time of availability. Typically, a three-week window is enough time for a client to make a decision and a fair enough window for you to be able to honor rates, promotions, etc.

Note: If you're presenting limited or first-come opportunities, make sure that is clearly noted in the proposal. Fear of loss is a powerful motivator.

Avoid these 10 common proposal mistakes and you'll have more effective presentations.

CHAPTER 10

DON'T FORGET THE LAUNCH PARTY!

ORIGINALLY PUBLISHED: 12/2/2006

2020 Perspective – For the past few years, I've been cautioning to "Beware the Last Mile!" My definition of the Last Mile is the initial touchpoint between our advertiser and their prospect. I've seen way too many good advertising campaigns derailed by a poorly designed website or an ill-prepared frontliner who doesn't answer the phone correctly. Use the Launch Party to rally the frontliners and train them to react properly when you drive those valuable leads!

Twice in the past month, I've witnessed the incredibly positive effect of the Pre-Launch Kick Off Party during the sales presentation. If you're missing this step in the sales process, you're missing a critical element.

On the Next Steps page of your presentation, you talk about copy approval, production deadlines, and other elements that need to be addressed before the campaign can start. One of the elements we preach is the pre-launch kickoff meeting. We highly recommend hosting a gathering of the client's staff to introduce the campaign, show the spot, and get everyone internally fired up for the launch of the advertising campaign.

Sometimes, we quickly gloss over this element of the action steps, or worse yet, we fail to include it altogether. Big mistake. Let me share two specific instances that happened to me in the past month that prove the value of highlighting the pre-launch kickoff meeting.

The first happened while presenting a large proposal to a casino. The client seemed moderately engaged throughout the presentation. When we got to the Next Steps, we offered to host a kickoff breakfast to be held in a hospitality room at the casino. We described a pleasant breakfast spread that would be opened to the entire casino staff. At the breakfast, station representatives would be on hand to introduce the new creative, describe the campaign, and answer any questions. Pretty typical, right? Well, as soon as we presented this element, the clients got all excited. It seems there had been some internal conflict between the different departments at the casino, and the client saw our breakfast meeting as a great opportunity to bring everyone together in a positive way. From that point forward, our presentation took on a new level of energy and likelihood.

The next instance occurred at a senior living facility. During the entire presentation, the clients offered little feedback as we outlined strategy and creative. When we got to the Next Steps page, we kind of glossed over the kickoff meeting. Luckily, one of the station representatives in the meeting made it a point to go back to the kickoff meeting bullet point and reiterate its value. At that point, the clients really understood the benefit. They began to discuss amongst themselves how to incorporate all the shifts so everyone could participate. Once again, the meeting took on a whole new level of excitement.

If you're missing this step or not giving it it's due in your presentations, I urge you to remind yourself of the value. Trust me, no other competitor is including this step in their proposals. It will really make you stand out.

Here's a bonus idea. Why not invite the client to a "News and Dinner" reception at your station? You invite the client to come to the TV station for the first airing of their commercial in your local news. Have a dinner catered in, take the client on a tour of the station, introduce the news talent, and enjoy a dinner while watching the newscast. Have a toast when the spot runs!

CHAPTER 11

PROCEED, PROCEED WITH CHANGES, STOP THE PROCESS

ORIGINALLY PUBLISHED: 5/12/2010

2020 Perspective – This is still the easiest closing tool I've ever seen. Proceed, Proceed with Changes or Stop the Process. When I deliver the Proceed with Changes option, I'll say, "And if we need to make some adjustments, like tweak the copy, you can decide to Proceed with Changes..." I say it that way to deflect the change away from the investment level.

In our proposal template, we have created our "closing page." It's simply a page/slide that says:

Proceed
Proceed with Changes
Stop the Process

This is followed by a timeline of events such as copy approval, production completed, meet with staff for a launch party, etc.

I've been using this closing page for about two years now and have never used such an easy, effective closing tool. At the conclusion of the presentation, after we've delivered the strategy, the creative idea, the schedule, and the price tag (along with any closing incentives), I simply say, "That's what we're excited to present to you today and you have 3 options. If we hit the nail on the head, we can proceed. If we need to make some changes, like tweaking the copy, we can proceed with changes, or if we completely missed the boat, we can stop the process. Which would you like to do?"

Done.

That's it. Mouth shut, wait for the answer.

Here's the beauty of this closing page. Sometimes the prospect chooses Proceed. Most of the time they choose Proceed with Changes. Almost never do they choose Stop the Process. So, in almost all cases, you are Proceeding towards your goal—a "yes."

Recently, I learned of a station that altered our closing page. They felt "Stop the Process" was too negative, too final. So, they changed it to "Go Back to the Drawing Board," as a way to soften it up and still be in the game if the client chose not to Proceed or Proceed with Changes.

I disagree with that strategy. Here's why: clients almost never choose Stop the Process, but when they do, you should probably stop the process! The few times a client has told me they wanted to stop the process, they usually had bad circumstances surrounding them. They either owed money, were being sued, or were considering closing, selling or something similar. Every once in a while, they just don't believe in your product, strategy or value. For those few, I really don't want to "go back to the drawing board." I'd rather cut my losses and focus my time elsewhere.

Here's the other reason I disagree with "Go Back to the Drawing Board" replacing "Stop the Process" as an option: "Go Back to the Drawing Board" is a viable option for someone who could have said, "Proceed with Changes," and I'd much rather have them say, "Proceed with Changes." In other words, given the choice between "Proceed with Changes" and "Go Back to the Drawing Board," some clients who could be saying "Proceed with Changes" will take "Go Back to the Drawing Board." It means you have to start all over with those clients, as opposed to moving forward with identifiable changes and not having to scrap all of your work.

38

A client who agrees to Proceed with Changes is much closer to a sale than the client who agrees to Go Back to the Drawing Board.

I bet the station that changed the offer from "Stop the Process" to "Go Back to the Drawing Board" is losing a whole bunch of clients who would have chosen "Proceed with Changes."

Don't fear the "Stop the Process" option.

CHAPTER 12

PROSPECTING POINT SYSTEM

ORIGINALLY PUBLISHED: 8/17/2008

2020 Perspective – I wrote this article for our Leader's Edge management newsletter in the summer of 2008 when the need to create new business to replace the cancellations was peaking. Any manager or AE can easily and quickly prioritize their new biz efforts with this simple 30-point scale.

Have you ever had an account executive spend months working a "hot prospect" only to find out the potential client has no money? Or the AE who invests lots of time in a prospect who has zero desire to advertise? With the enhanced focus on new business during these challenging conditions, better prospecting has become more and more important. As managers, we need to make sure our AE's are prospecting, and prospecting wisely.

From our manager's chair, it may sometimes be difficult to feel confident that our reps, particularly our younger "new business development" players, are spending their time in front of the right prospects.

Here's a simple system to help qualify the prospect list. It's a 30-point system based on 3 simple criteria.

On a scale of 1 to 10, rate each prospect for the following: Need, Desire, Budget.

Need – how badly does the prospect need your product? Do you have demonstrable success in this prospect's category? Granted, we can and should make a case for every business needing to advertise. But, for this exercise, quantify on the 1 to 10 scale an honest answer to the need question. So, a brand-new dental practice with zero market recognition would score much higher than the mature practice that has a 3-month wait for new patients. How badly does the business NEED to advertise?

Desire – how much desire does the prospect have for your product? Lots of businesses have a high degree of need in our eyes, but very low desire to do anything about it. Obviously, a better prospect to spend your time with is one who wants to do something about their need! Remember the farmer and the tractor salesman story? The farmer, in obvious need of a new tractor, keeps telling the tractor salesman it's not a good time because "my dog is dying." When the tractor salesman protests, the farmer says, "When I ain't buyin', one excuse is as good as the next." That's the classic example of zero desire.

Budget – Do they have the resources to do anything about their need? How many times have your AE's spun their wheels with a prospect who needs to advertise, wants to advertise, but has no means to do anything? Determine if there is a budget, and if so, what size.

As you sit with your AE's, ask them to go through each prospect they're working on and rate each of these 3 criteria on a scale of 1 to 10 to determine a "grade." It's a simple way to prioritize where they should be spending their time and efforts. And, it's a quick way to help new AE's qualify between real prospects and suspects.

CHAPTER 13

ALWAYS HAVE A BIG PROJECT

ORIGINALLY PUBLISHED: 5/3/2007

2020 Perspective – So, what is something big that you're working on right now? Are you proud of your answer? If not, then it's time to create a big project!

Many years ago, I worked with an excellent AE. He was one of those guys who not only hit budget consistently but managed to turn heads a few times a year with an "Oh Wow" sale. You know what I'm talking about—the sale that transcends the transactional, the sale that no one else in the market was even calling on. When I asked him how he did it, he shared one of his simple rules. He said, "You always gotta have a big project you're working on..."

How simple. To regularly produce "Oh Wow!" sales, always have a big project you're working on. Allow me to clarify. Big projects are NOT station-driven, they're AE-driven. What I mean is, taking your NFL package out is not a big project. Big projects are generated by the specific Account Executive for themselves. It is their own idea, something they want to work on, not a required package. They create the idea, build it from scratch, and bring it to their own prospects and clients. It is nontraditional.

How many on your sales team always have a Big Project they're working on? It's a great question to ask each seller during their one-on-one with you. Regularly ask, "What is something BIG you're working on?" The answer could tell you volumes about their future success. If you get an enthusiastic answer that details a unique idea they've created, you're probably sitting with a winner. If you get a "deer in the headlights" stare, you have some work to do. Don't accept "Well, I'm trying to get this guy on" as an answer. What you're looking for is something non-traditional, multi-platform, and groundbreaking.

Here's why I believe AE-driven big projects are important:

- **Big projects energize!** When you have something exciting to work on, your energy increases.
- **They develop category expertise.** Big projects enable in-depth learning in chosen categories.
- **They fill the AE's downtime.** When the AE has that extra half hour in their day, they have something they're excited about working on.
- **They create a focus.** Sometimes AE's invest in time-wasting busy work. A big project gives them direction and opportunity to better prioritize their days.
- **They establish momentum.** When the AE is busy, engaged and energized, momentum carries over to everything else they're doing.

Ask the question, "What is something BIG you're working on?" It shows your staff that you expect big new business development... from everyone. It tells the AE's that they're capable of creating their own BIG projects. Make sure you help them cut through the station red tape. Tell them that if they sell their idea, you'll figure out how to make it happen internally.

Encourage everyone to think grand scale, out-of-the-box, nontraditional, multi-platform, different, independent, unique, complex... In fishing, there's a saying, "To catch BIG fish, you gotta use BIG bait." Your AE's need to come up with BIG ideas to go sell the BIG project.

CHAPTER 14

WINNING BUSINESS FROM A COMPETITOR... WHAT DOES IT TAKE?

ORIGINALLY PUBLISHED: 6/22/2008

2020 Perspective – There will never be a better time to switch pitch than right now! When it's "the worst I've ever seen," it's time to attack. Target those relationships that may have gone stale, the one's where the AE has taken a client for granted for too long. Right now, all's fair in love, war, and media sales!

Do you have any prospective client targeted who's "in tight" with a competitor? Someone who you know is spending a lot elsewhere and would really benefit from a partnership with your station? What does it take to win that kind of business?

I was thinking about that while I was flying on an airline that I typically don't fly. I'm a frequent flyer and I'm very loyal to one major airline. On this particular trip, my regular carrier was unable to accommodate me, so I had to use their competitor. I wondered what it would take to get me to switch all my business to this airline.

In today's economic climate, all relationships are vulnerable. Meaning, those bonds that seemed unbreakable are worth approaching.

I'm very happy with the airline to which I've been loyal. They treat me well, give me rewards, and I've achieved a certain status with them. But, I also know I'm a good customer that lots of their competitors would like to have.

There are advertisers in your market who feel the same way. They're not unhappy with their current partnerships, but they'd entertain proposals. Now is the time to target those prospects. Every advertiser is questioning, more than ever, each of their advertising partnerships.

Here are some of the things they WON'T switch for:

1. Higher ratings
2. Lower Cost Per Point
3. More spots

None of these in and of themselves is enough to get a satisfied advertiser away from their current partner. That would be like the competing airline coming to me and saying, "Switch to us because we have better on time arrival ratings, a higher customer satisfaction index, and we're usually $10 lower on most comparable fares!"

Thanks, but no thanks. It ain't enough. Again, I'm not dissatisfied with my current situation.

When you get in front of an advertiser who is relatively happy with what they're doing, your 3.6 rating compared to the competition's 3.0 in the 6pm News isn't a Tipping Point.

What does it take? It takes a Big Idea. Bring the client something big that your competitor can't or hasn't offered. Rational doesn't work to shift major dollars. What works is an emotional pull. Think really big when going after a client who is loyal to a competitor. Don't focus on the rational—the ratings and rates stuff—what I like to call "the math." Instead, open their eyes with a big idea: exclusive partnerships, promotions, contesting, incentives.

Mind you, switching a satisfied client over to you isn't cheap. The cost of sale to win business can be dramatic. You have to decide what it's worth on your end to even go after the business. And, when you do, you must present to the decision-maker. Trying to make a major shift with anyone other than the ultimate decision-maker is an exercise in futility.

Here's one more thing to consider... a brilliant colleague of mine once said that, "relationships are not linear." He meant that most salespeople make the mistake of believing that their relationship with a client always grows over time. It doesn't. Anyone who has been selling media for a number of years knows that clients can, and will, jump ship on you. Alliances are vulnerable this year... did you see *Survivor* this season?

Think big, think exclusive, think "what can we offer that their current partner can't?" Don't waste a lot of effort on the rational. Focus on the emotional and make sure you only present to the decision-maker.

CHAPTER 15

WHAT'S YOUR "ALLIGATOR SPEECH?"

ORIGINALLY PUBLISHED: 7/1/2010

2020 Perspective – "You" is still greater than "Me." And, I still haven't had to outrun a gator!

I know! Shouldn't that be "Elevator Speech?" That two-minute, well-crafted response to the question, "So what do you do?" Imagine you're in an elevator and have just two minutes to deliver your message most effectively to your captive audience. The idea of an "elevator speech" is to have a prepared presentation that grabs attention and says a lot in a few words. What are you going to say? By telling your core message, you will be marketing yourself and/or your business, but in a way that rather than putting people off, will make them want to know more about you and your business.

Recently, a sales manager friend from a TV station asked me if I had any great examples of the perfect elevator speech. He was working with his staff on crafting the perfect speech for the team. The sales manager also sent me the examples his team had put together. That's when it struck me! After reading what his team submitted, I replied with the following:

I, I, I, I, I...

I help local businesses...
I work at WXYZ...
I'm an Account Executive...
I'm in the business of success...
I'm a multimedia consultant...

I, I, I, I, I...

Shouldn't it be about You, You, You?

Get the book, *POP! Stand Out in Any Crowd* by Sam Horn. She talks about elevator pitches in several sections of the book.

I interviewed her for our Achiever's Circle group earlier this year. Basically, when it comes to an elevator pitch for an AE, she suggested we choose a widely recognized local success story client and use them as the basis of our pitch. As in, "Do you know the furniture commercial 'gotta go downer!' with the guy who hits the onions? Well, that's what I do. I help local businesses find their unique value proposition and then help them creatively bring that message to their customers and prospects..."

It's not about "I," it's about "You."

That's why I prefer openings like: *Do YOU know the Smith Dry Cleaner commercial that talks about being Perc Free?*

Or,

Have YOU ever seen the Home of the Half Price Car commercial?

Or even

Do YOU watch local television news? Well, I'm the person who helps businesses deliver their message to YOU while YOU are watching...

I do think things like "I'm in the business of success..." and "I help local businesses make more money..." are better than "I'm an Account Executive," but ask your team if they'd really ever answer someone who asked, "So what do you do?" by saying, "I'm in the business of success..." Would they really say that? But they would easily say, "Do you watch local news on TV? Well..."

Now here's why I want to change it from Elevator Speech to Alligator Speech: Who has an uninterrupted two minutes to listen to anyone answer the question, "So what do you do?"

NOBODY! We force ourselves to have a perfectly crafted two minutes that will only ever be delivered in its entirety in a sales meeting with our colleagues! So, why an Alligator Speech? I just moved to Florida and am getting acquainted with alligators. I recently learned that if an alligator chases you, you should run in a straight line as fast as you can. After 35 yards or so, the lactic acid will begin to build up in the gator and they will give up on you. So, rather than perfecting a two-minute elevator speech, I say perfect a 35-second alligator speech! What would you say in only 35 seconds that would be delivered with all the energy and intensity of an alligator attack? Say something so cool that it grabs your audience and won't let go.

Here's a little secret... people develop elevator speeches to try to make their boring jobs or mundane products seem appealing. Well guess what? If you're in TV or radio, people already think that's cool! Now, take that coolness and make if beneficial to the person you're addressing, and remember, it's about them, not you.

CHAPTER 16

OVERCOMING THE WOM ROADBLOCK

ORIGINALLY PUBLISHED: 11/15/2008

2020 Perspective – Wow! More than ever, you can help a business harness the power of word of mouth! Your digital toolkit is loaded with ways to enhance community, reviews, social media... word of mouth. I think "word of mouth" has gone from one of the most feared responses to one of the most welcome!

Has this ever happened to you? You're in the middle of a good Time Out Call, you've identified everywhere the client is spending their advertising dollars, and then you ask, "Of all the advertising you do, what works best?" The client smiles slyly, and as if to say "Gotcha!" replies, "You know what works best for me... Word of Mouth."

In the client's mind, word of mouth translates to "you can't help me." They throw it out there to stop you dead in your tracks, to knock you off your game, to take control of the meeting.

Clients typically define word of mouth as the referrals and exchanges that occur between customers and prospects. It's what happens outside of their business. And, in most cases, clients don't associate any other outside advertising with word of mouth, so they think you can't help them affect it. They truly believe that even though they may spend tens of thousands in advertising, you could throw it all away because this uncontrollable beast called word of mouth is what really drives new customers and there's nothing anyone can do from an advertising perspective to drive it, generate it or affect it.

As account executives, do we tuck our tail between our legs and agree that word of mouth is awesome and we "really can't help you there, but, as a secondary option, would you consider my product?" Do we simply gloss over the word of mouth comment and say, "Yeah, but of the paid stuff, what works?" Or, "Other than word of mouth, if you had to choose something else, what would it be?"

Here's how I suggest you handle the word of mouth objection...

When a client throws word of mouth at me, I now immediately reply, "That's GREAT! How are you controlling it?" Just as the client thinks they've thrown you a curve ball, this is a back-at-you response. Inevitably, the client will say, "What do you mean" because in their mind one cannot control word of mouth. I'll repeat my question, "How are you controlling word of mouth? Are you blogging? Email marketing? Do you do something remarkable? What reasons are you giving people to talk about you? How are you controlling it?"

The client will struggle with this because, again, they believe one cannot control word of mouth. They are wrong!

In his book *Word of Mouth Marketing – How Smart Companies Get People Talking*, author Andy Sernovitz (CEO of the Word of Mouth Marketing Association) says, "Your job as marketer is to put out an idea worth talking about. The more you participate, the more the conversation grows, and the more it is about you. Feed it! Put the good stuff out there." Says Sernovitz, "Traditional media and word of mouth are forever intertwined."

It is our job to help the client understand that advertising is the most powerful way to create, control and sustain word of mouth. We need to build the bridge between creating a marketing message and having it affect what people are saying about a business.

Next time a client throws word of mouth at you, smile and understand it is no longer a "stop you in your tracks" objection, but an opportunity to help the client learn how to control what is being said about their business.

CHAPTER 17

"I'LL GIVE YOU 15 MINUTES"

ORIGINALLY PUBLISHED: 2/10/2015

2020 Perspective – In these chaotic conditions, you'd better be prepared, be brief, and bring value to every interaction. Make it about them, not you!

"Talk to people about themselves, and they will listen for hours" -Benjamin Disraeli

We recently received this email from a frantic AE...

Hi everyone, can you help me? I have an appt in the a.m. tomorrow and they're only giving me 15 minutes. What specifically should I ask?

Here's what I replied...

First, I'd do all the upfront research I could...
- *Deep dive into their website*
- *Google the business*
- *Google the owner*
- *GoogleNews the business and owner*
- *Facebook explore to see what their community is talking about*
- *LinkedIn*
- *Twitter*

All the upfront research allows you to have answers to many of your diagnosis basics, so you don't have to waste time on those. In fact, I'd say, "I researched your website, your Google presence, your Facebook, LinkedIn, and Twitter presence in advance of this meeting. So, unless there's some unique circumstance, I'm not going to spend a lot of time on the basics..."

Or some sort of statement that gives you credit for the strong upfront work.

Here are some questions I love that cannot be answered by a website review:

How are you perceived in the marketplace? In other words, if I asked 100 people around town, "What do you think of when you hear the name (insert business name)? What would the market tell me?" Followed up with, *"So how would you like to be perceived?"*

I would definitely want them to describe their target. *"How would you describe your core customer / patient / client / prospect?"*

I would want to hear from them how they perceive the competitive landscape, followed by (and this is probably the MOST important question you could ask) *"So, why then, should I come see you?"* If I only have 15 minutes, I want to make sure I uncover their USP—their "one thing"!!

Keep the pleasantries to a minimum. I'd start by saying something like, *"I know our time is limited today, so if you don't mind, I'd like to just jump right in..."*

Finally, and I'm sure you've personally experienced this, I've been in many meetings that were limited to 15 minutes and walked out after an hour! If they're engaged, they'll give you time. If you come as a package seller and it's all "me, me, me," you'll be escorted to the door in 15 minutes. But, if it's all about them, they'll talk.

CHAPTER 18

IT'S TIME TO REALLY FOCUS ON ROI

ORIGINALLY PUBLISHED: 9/6/2008

2020 Perspective – ROI is more critical than ever, especially in a challenged environment. And, with our digital tools allowing for even greater accountability, we have every opportunity to demonstrate ROI.

Part I: The Questions

Now, more than ever before, we must focus on Return on Investment during our selling efforts.

How many times have we "sold" a client a schedule or campaign, and then crossed our fingers and hoped that the client is happy with what happens? We have no accountability or measurement in place and we're not really sure what has to happen as a result of our campaign to consider it a success. Current economic conditions are forcing everyone, from large corporations to smaller privately held companies, to maximize their revenue streams from new and existing customers. To be successful, firms today must outsell their competition and exceed customer expectations, thus creating long-term satisfaction and loyalty. ROI needs to be part of your solution, and a demonstrable ROI will win you more clients.

How do you go about ROI selling? First, you need to ask the right questions to gain the information used in setting up the accountability systems. Here's what you need to know...

What is the average ticket? Every good business owner should know what their average sale is. Specifically, it's calculated by dividing gross sales by the number of sales over a given period.

What is the weekly traffic? First, you must define traffic. What will you be measured against? Traffic can be measured in terms of prospects through the door, by phone or even website visitors. We need to benchmark the traffic. In an average week, how many customers will walk in? How many patients will you see? How many phone calls will you field? How many visitors to your website?

What is the closing percentage? Out of 10 "door pulls," how many will you close? Out of 10 phone inquiries, how many will turn into new patients? Out of 100 website visitors, how many will purchase online?

What is your margin on the average sale? Frankly, how much does the advertiser make in profit on a new sale?

What is the annual value of a new customer? Will a first-time customer typically buy more in year one? How much will each new customer spend with your business in the first year?

What is the lifetime value of a new customer? How much does each new customer typically represent in total lifetime expenditures with your company?

If these questions aren't part of your Time Out Call, you need to incorporate them now. Next, we will show you how to use this information to demonstrate a Return on Investment for your client.

Part II: Calculating ROI
- What is your average ticket?
- What is your weekly traffic?
- What is your closing percentage?
- What is your margin?
- What is the annual value of a new customer?
- What is the lifelong value of a new customer?

Now, what do you do with that information once you've uncovered it in a Time Out Call?

56

We need to show the client what needs to happen in order to justify the investment in your proposed campaign. Let's look at a couple of examples.

Example 1: Tiffany Furniture is a locally owned furniture store that sells Ashley, La-Z-Boy, etc.

- Average sale: $800
- Weekly traffic: 150 "ups" per week
- Closing ratio of 20%

So, we can determine from this information that they're averaging 30 sales per week, at around $24K-a-week gross sales. That's about $100K per month, making them a $1M-a-year store.

Let's say their margin is 40%, so they're making about $320 per sale (40% of the average sale of $800).

The annual value of a new customer is $800 (they typically only see a customer once a year).

The lifelong value of the customer is $4,000 (typically a customer will make a total of 5 purchases over their lifetime).

So, if we present a schedule at $4,000 per month, what has to happen?

We'll need to generate 12.5 new sales to cover the investment. We determined this by dividing the advertising investment by the average profit per sale ($4,000 divided by $320 = 12.5).

We know the closing ratio is 20%, so we would have to deliver just over 60 new door pulls per month (60 door pulls x 20% = 12 sales).

Is it reasonable to assume that we can expect 15 new door pulls per week (or 2.5 new door pulls per day) from our proposed schedule, which will reach x% of the market (or 80,000 women, 35-64)?

And... if we achieve 12 new sales per month, we're talking $48,000 in lifelong revenue from those clients.

Does that justify the $4,000 monthly investment?

Let try another example: Smith Dental wants to own

the sedation dentistry position.
- Average Sedation Case: $2,000
- Currently 40 new patient calls per month.
- Closing ratio of 50%.
- So, they're currently generating 20 new patients per month.
- The profit on the average sedation case is $800.
- The first-year value of the sedation patient is $1,000 in profit. They need to come back in 6 months for a checkup.
- The lifelong value of the sedation patient is $10,000. A dental patient is of very high lifetime value, especially a sedation patient.

So, if we present a $5,000 per month schedule, what has to happen?

We'll need to generate 10 new inquiries per month. We determine this by dividing the monthly investment by the first-year value of a new patient ($5,000 divided by $1,000 = 5). We know we need to generate 10 calls with a 50% close ratio to achieve our 5 new patients.

Is it reasonable to assume that we can generate 10 calls per month from our $5,000 schedule, which will reach x% of the market (or 100,000 adults 25-54)?

And... with a lifelong value of $10,000, each new patient covers 2 months of advertising investment.

It's a matter of gaining the information and being able to show the math that justifies the investment.

Now, add on top of that the branding, name recognition, and forward equity that are also benefits of advertising and the investment becomes even more justifiable.

CHAPTER 19

"I'M NOT DOING ANYTHING RIGHT NOW!"

ORIGINALLY PUBLISHED: 12/11/2008

<u>2020 Perspective</u> – Look, in the darkest of times, it may be a necessity for a business to suspend their advertising. We can tout until we're blue in the face how businesses that maintain their advertising gain market share at recovery. Fine. Try to tell that to someone who just furloughed their staff. Some healthy companies may be able to spend their way through, but many can't. The biggest mistake an advertiser will make is to cut everybody back by the same percentage. The much smarter move is to eliminate underperforming partners and keep the best performing partners at the highest level possible. If your client has to go dark, make sure you stay close so you can help them regain momentum when they're ready.

It's happening. Many clients have decided to just sit on the sidelines "until things get better." We're all hearing things like...

"I'm not doing anything right now."

"We're gonna go dark for a while."

"I've cancelled everything."

"I'm thinking about pulling off."

Here are some of my favorite responses, sayings, and analogies to share with the advertiser who wants to go dark...

"There is only one way to coast..." Let the client finish this one in their head— "Downhill!"

I have added the following question to my Time Out Calls, "What would happen if you did nothing at all?" Just so I can hear the client admit that doing nothing will absolutely not make things BETTER. Then I share that back with them in the presentation.

"Running a business without advertising is like winking at someone in the dark—you know you're doing it, but no one else does!"

Here's how I typically respond to the advertiser who wants to pull off for a while...

"Advertising is like pushing a car that's run out of gas. It takes the greatest amount of energy and effort at the very beginning to get that car rolling. But once you've built a little momentum, it gets easier to maintain a pace. In fact, even if you let go—i.e. stop advertising—the car will still roll a little longer, but eventually it will come to a complete stop. Then, you'll have to use all that energy and effort just to get it rolling again. I'd hate to see you lose all the momentum you've established by completely pulling off."

You need to make sure the client understands the consequences of going dark. The above thoughts may help them re-think their decisions.

BONUS: If you don't like the "car out of gas" analogy, try changing it to "pushing my child in a swing." The first push is the hardest, but then I just need to give a gentle push each time to keep her going. If, however, I stop pushing all together, she'll continue to swing for a while and eventually will come to a complete stop. Then, I'll have to give that first big push just to get her started again.

CHAPTER 20

PAWNED OFF ON SOMEBODY ELSE, WHAT DO YOU DO?

ORIGINALLY PUBLISHED: 12/11/2009

2020 Perspective – You're going to get stiffed on meetings. You're going to get pawned off to others. Gather as much information as you can, from whomever you can. But never give a proposal to someone who can't say yes!

You had the meeting planned for three weeks. You sent a confirmation. You stopped to pick up bagels. You're prepared and ready and you show up as scheduled, only to get stiffed by the person you know is the ultimate decision-maker!

What do you do when you show up for a meeting that you had scheduled with the ultimate decision-maker and, for whatever reason, they toss you to someone else?

I think your next move depends on what type of meeting it is. Let's start with the **Time Out Call**...

When the ultimate decision-maker tosses you to someone else, I say, go ahead with the meeting. You're there, you made the effort, and at least someone from an organization you're trying to learn more about is willing to talk to you. Recently, I showed up for a scheduled Time Out Call appointment with a cosmetic dentist. Upon arrival, the office manager greeted us and told us the doctor was unable to meet personally, but that she, the office manager, could answer our questions. Although disappointed, we took advantage of the opportunity to ask some questions. Surprisingly, the office manager was very capable of handling most of our questions and the meeting was very productive. It also gave us the chance to develop a "coach," using a term from Robert Miller and Stephen Heiman's book, *Strategic Selling*.

The other phenomenon that sometimes occurs is that the Ultimate Decision-Maker Stand-in doesn't know what NOT to say, so they can be a wealth of information that the ultimate decision-maker may not divulge.

Now, when it comes to the **Presentation...**

If you have a scheduled appointment with the ultimate decision-maker and they stiff you and push you off to someone else, **Don't Do It!** Do not deliver your presentation! Ask to re-schedule.

Here's why: If you're there for a presentation with the ultimate decision-maker, you have one goal... walk out with the order. Why would your goal be anything else? By definition, the ultimate decision-maker is the **only one** who can say "yes." In a presentation, you're going to ask for the business, so expect that you'll leave with a deal. If they pawn you off on someone else, you cannot leave with an agreement to proceed. So, don't do it!

A few months back, I showed up to a business with a homerun idea wrapped inside a well-conceived presentation. The business owner was out at a customer appointment and couldn't meet with us. She asked us to give the presentation to her manager. I declined.

I said to the manager, "I am so excited about what we've developed for your business that I want to present it to Mary (the owner) myself! Can we reschedule for later today or tomorrow when Mary can be available too?"

We did, it sold. It was a nice way of telling the manager that with all due respect, I did not want to rely on him to move my presentation forward.

You may be excited about your presentation and ideas and want to share them as soon as you can with whomever you can. Resist that urge. You may think that the manager (who may even be a "coach") can help sell this up. Don't do it. Don't trial-run your proposal to get their feedback. Hold off. If the ultimate decision-maker had agreed to see you, make them honor the commitment. The results are worth the wait.

CHAPTER 21

TOUGH TIMES MAKE FOR TOUGH BUYERS

ORIGINALLY PUBLISHED: 7/25/2009

2020 Perspective – It's the toughest we've ever seen it. Right now. Time to re-write our own playbook and get creative. We may have to do things we've never considered, just like our advertisers are having to do things and make offers they've never considered. In fact, as I write this, I just received an email from the President of Delta Airlines informing me that my current 2020 status will be extended through all of 2021, and I'll be getting a six-month free extension on my Delta Sky Club membership. Wow! That's a proactive, above-and-beyond reaction to our current climate from one of the hardest hit categories. Is it any wonder I'll continue to fly Delta almost exclusively?

Here are 4 things you can do to deal with those tough buyers...

Demonstrate ROI – Make ROI a regular piece to all of your presentations. Be sure you're getting all the necessary information in your Time Out Call...

- average sale
- closing ratio
- profit margin

That way, you can put together an ROI slide and show how your plan will deliver a return.

Bring "big ideas" – A hot idea melts a cold objection every time. Every proposal should have some sort of "big idea." It could be in the form of creative (a well-crafted script or spec), it could be promotional in nature (a station or third party tie-in), it could be strategic (a sponsorship or results-oriented strategy like "own a night"), but every proposal should rest on a "big idea."

Be proactive – Don't wait for the buyer to contact you. Be proactive in generating an opportunity. Be proactive in addressing problems. Be proactive in delivering exceptional service.

Offer "unheard of" incentives – Let's face it, everyone is looking to get more for less in this new economy. I love how John Jantsch puts it in *Duct Tape Marketing*:

"Create an astonishing offer—one that makes you nervous—and that's the point. If you could create and communicate an offer that nobody in your industry would even consider, you would automatically have two very powerful things going for you: a core marketing message that would differentiate you from your competition, and a forced focus on delivering excellence and winning loyal, repeat customers. An astonishing offer turns heads, an astonishing offer generates buzz, an astonishing offer creates a mission."

I know what you're saying... "I'm not just gonna give away my inventory." Well, that's not what I'm saying. I'm saying offer "unheard of" incentives. That doesn't necessarily mean FREE SPOTS. If you don't normally include free production, then maybe that's what you focus on. Or maybe you could include sponsorships you don't necessarily give away. Be creative, think outside the box, come up with something that you've not regularly offered as an incentive (maybe a deep discount for early pay or cash in advance!). The point is, give the tough buyer something to chew on in the form of an incentive.

Tough times make for tough buyers. It's up to you to get better and make it easier for the tough buyer to partner with you instead of your competition.

CHAPTER 22

YOUR PRESENTATION BEGINS BEFORE YOU OPEN YOUR MOUTH

ORIGINALLY PUBLISHED: 5/3/2010

2020 Perspective – Today, more than ever, Big Brother is always watching. Everything you do from the moment you arrive at a prospect is being monitored. Nonverbals matter. Always act like the Pro that you are, respect everyone, and you'll have nothing to worry about.

I'll never forget years ago, as a relative newbie in the media sales business, I had just finished a presentation with my manager. We were at one of the larger agencies in town and we presented a promotional idea for one of their clients. The presentation went okay, but one of the agency people in the room was unimpressed and we just didn't connect.

On the elevator ride down, I made a comment to my manager about the call. I was looking for some feedback and got nothing. I thought she must be really upset with my performance. It wasn't until we got in the car and drove away that she told me she didn't respond to my question because the other person in the elevator with us was the business manager for the agency. I had no idea!

And, did you see the video of the British politician who was unaware his microphone was still on as he drove away from an appearance. He made some derogatory comments about one of the attendees and within hours it was on the Internet.

Your presentation doesn't begin when you start your PowerPoint in the conference room. Your presentation begins the moment your car hits the client's parking lot. Someone is watching where you park (make it a habit to NEVER take a good parking spot that could go to a customer!), how you approach, what you say to the receptionist. Your communication begins sooner than you think.

Remember those auto execs arriving in their private planes to ask for taxpayer money last year?

I follow these simple rules...

- I always park away from the client's building, leaving the good spots for customers
- I greet everyone with a smile
- I don't assume any roles. As far as I am concerned, everyone is the CEO
- I mind my manners, I hold the door for people, and say "please" and "thank you"
- I never show reaction to a call until I'm in my car and driving away. (How would you feel if you saw someone who just sold you something high-fiving with his manager?!)

Remember, you are always "on."

Chapter 23

Rehearse, Rehearse, Rehearse!

Originally Published: 9/11/2008

2020 Perspective – *I've done lots more presentations since I originally wrote this article for our Achiever's Circle newsletter in 2008. I've since become a member of the National Speakers Association and have earned my Certified Speaking Professional designation. I know the importance of rehearsal. You MUST rehearse. And today, we're recommending that you do as many presentations as you can in your conference room. It's called "Home Field Advantage" for a reason.*

I'm also convinced that moving forward, we'll be doing more and more presentations virtually. Those of us who embrace video presenting will have an advantage.

Imagine a Grammy Award winning artist composing the next great song. It's a complex number filled with overlapping harmonies and an amazing hook that's sure to be a hit. How many times do you think it will be rehearsed before it's ever performed in front of the buying audience?

Well, consider your next big presentation to be as important as an award-winning composition. It's got different layers, a sound strategy, and an amazing creative idea that everyone will be talking about. There's too much at stake to perform it "live" for the first time without any rehearsal.

It's the season of the annual presentation. Lots of proposals are being created and presented for 2009 annual commitments. It's a great time to remind ourselves that we need to be rehearsing our presentations before we get in front of the client.

We've harped on the fact that the days of "winging it" are over. At no time is that more apparent than in the presentation stage. When you've spent hours building your strategy into a rock-solid presentation, make sure you're fully prepared and well-rehearsed to maximize your efforts.

Here are the things to consider:
- Who will be presenting? Will you be the only presenter or will someone else join you, such as a manager? Do you each know your role and who's going to handle which part of the presentation?
- Where will you be presenting? What are the surroundings? What can you control and what can't you control?
- What tools will you have available? Will you be presenting via laptop, projector or paper?
- Who will you be presenting to?

Dry-run the presentation in your conference room with your sales manager. Do this a few days before the client presentation to allow time to revise and re-rehearse. Ask your manager to allow you to present to your teammates in your weekly sales meeting to get even more feedback.

What about mistakes that happen during your presentation? My friend, Ted, is a professional musician. He said to me recently, "I like making mistakes, it gives me a chance to improvise!" I love that attitude and will think of him the next time I make a mistake during a presentation. If I'm well-rehearsed, a mistake won't fluster me or throw me off my game. It will simply give me the opportunity to improvise a little before I get back on track.

A well-rehearsed presentation is one that's delivered with confidence, enthusiasm and power, and will dramatically increase the chances of success.

CHAPTER 24

SELLING IS MORE LIKE JAZZ THAN A SYMPHONY!

ORIGINALLY PUBLISHED: 4/14/2010

2020 Perspective – And it's still more like jazz... Jazz musicians rehearse, they are masterful at the fundamentals, they follow structure, and they are the best improvisors of all.

Jazz keyboardist, Herbie Hancock, tells the story of when he was performing with the legendary Miles Davis and hit a wrong chord. Davis paused briefly, looked at Herbie, then proceeded to deliver a blistering solo that made the chord work in the piece.

Selling is a lot like jazz. It's more free form than scripted, and improvising is allowed!

I was working with an AE recently who was much more of a symphonic performer than a jazz "artist." This AE was very talented—she knew her piece inside and out. She was well rehearsed. Problem was, she couldn't improvise.

She delivered her proposal exactly how she had written it and rehearsed it. However, when the client responded with an objection and hit a wrong chord, she continued to blast through her composition with no reaction to the change. Like a musician in the orchestra, she completely ignored what was happening around her and was totally focused on delivering her performance, as it was written and rehearsed.

The client said, "This looks fine, but I wouldn't be ready to start until the Fall." Instead of reacting to that new piece of information, the AE continued her presentation and delivered a special "this week only" signing incentive. It was rather awkward that the client had clearly said nothing was going to happen for months, yet she insisted on moving forward with the signing incentive. Don't get me wrong. I would have respected her had she said, "Is there anything we could do to get you to start sooner?" or some other sensible reaction to the put off. But it wasn't like that at all. She simply acted as if she didn't hear the objection and was clearly in the zone of "this is what I came to present, and by golly, I'm gonna present it!"

We need to be more like jazz musicians when we're selling. We need to be able to react accordingly when someone hits a wrong chord or gives us the nod to take a solo. We need to be involved and listening and taking cues, not just reading our script, oblivious to the conditions around us. While the symphony plays the same piece, night after night, the same way, the jazz group never plays the exact same performance. The songs may be the same, the order may be the same, even the solos may be in the same place, but something will be improvised.

Selling is more like jazz than the symphony.

CHAPTER 25

5 REASONS TO SCHEDULE TIME OUT CALLS WITH YOUR BIGGEST CLIENTS RIGHT NOW!

ORIGINALLY PUBLISHED: 8/16/2009

2020 Perspective – When conditions are adverse, businesses need to assess their advertising and may need to pivot to take advantage of circumstances or avoid mistakes. A full diagnosis call helps to uncover opportunities to pivot, and our digital tools are especially helpful, as they allow for quick creative pivots and things like A/B testing. Nine-Eleven. The Great Recession. Coronavirus. Regardless of the stimulus, all adverse downturns have a lifespan, and at the end of that downturn lifespan is some level of recovery. Adverse conditions are the perfect time to do a full Time Out Call with your clients who have been in fear mode. Be the first media partner to strategize a Recovery Plan for their business.

Here are 5 reasons why right now is the very best time to hold a full diagnosis call with your biggest and best clients.

1. **Annual season is fast approaching.** I always like to fill August and September with good, full Time Out Calls to get prepared for annual presentations for next year. In August and September, clients have a decent feel for how the current year will end and have started formulating their plans for the coming year. Get in front of them at this stage so you're in on the planning phase and can beat your competition to the punch.

2. **Recovery!** Most experts are telling us we've reached the bottom and things are picking up. Now is the perfect time to do a full Time Out Call with your clients who have been in fear mode for the past 18 months. Be the first media partner to strategize a Recovery Plan for their business.

3. **They're not currently doing anything.** There's no better time than when your clients have "gone dark" to ask for their time for a strong Time Out Call. Your competition slides away with their tail between their legs when the client says, "We're pulling back for now." You, on the other hand, are smart enough to embrace that as a signal to perform a full diagnosis so you can be proactive about getting them up and running again.

4. **The changes that have occurred in your market.** I don't know what changes, but I'm sure something has recently changed in the media landscape in your market. Surely, your local newspaper has had some changes, or maybe it's a radio group or station that has seen some shifts. Develop the story about the changing local media landscape and use it as an entry point to get in front of your biggest advertisers.

5. **It's ALWAYS a good time for a Time Out Call!** Bottom line, I have performed valuable Time Out Calls in every month of the year and discovered reasons to recommend good strategies and creative. Your business is changing, your clients' businesses are changing, the business climate is changing. You are a business partner. Get in front of your clients and strategize!

CHAPTER 26

YOU TOLD ME...

ORIGINALLY PUBLISHED: 11/8/2008

2020 Perspective – *I still vividly remember meeting the car dealer in Knoxville, TN, the first week of November 2008, when the proverbial shit hit the fan. Ever since, I've echoed his line, "The three most powerful words in sales are 'You told me.'" I truly believe it's the basis of the Jim Doyle & Associates UPGRADE Selling® System.*

I was recently delivering a very powerful station proposal to a car dealer. We were following our template and had some great ideas, both strategically and creatively. At the end of the presentation the dealer thanked us and commented on how good the presentation was. Then he looked at me and made a comment. "I loved the way you repeated my words back to me." He was referring to some direct quotes of his that I had included in the Current Situation page. He said, "I tell my salespeople all the time that the three most important words in the world are 'You told me...'" He had gone as far as to write the words "You told me" in the margin of the Current Situation page.

How powerful is the "you told me" tactic? Very. I use that technique all the time. I pepper my Current Situations with those great soundbites that I collect during the Time Out Call. In fact, sometimes those great soundbites turn into slogans for the client.

Later in the same week of presentations, a different client

said he tells his sales staff, "If you want to sell me something, listen to what I want to buy!"

So, how do we get really good soundbites to repeat back to our clients and prospects? We do it by asking really good, targeted questions and by listening intently. There's no doubt that the better the question, the juicier the answer.

When delivering your Current Situations, strive to include a direct quote or two. Frame it by saying, "I loved the way you said..." Or, "It really struck me when you shared...," and then serve the clients words back to them. As you deliver each bullet point of the Current Situation, say things like:

"You shared with me..."

"You said..."

"...and then I asked you ____, and you told me..."

Make the client take ownership of the content in the Current Situation. Then, tie your Recommended Strategy back to it.

Jim Doyle told me that if we nail the Current Situation right for a client who's in pain (and these days, who isn't?), they should be ready for a Prozac by the time we get to the end of it. We really need to listen and then deliver back the highlights of our Time Out Call.

Remember, the biggest "You told me..." of all is the title of your presentation. The very best presentation title is the specific answer to the Guru of Ads, Don Fitzgibbons's, Magic Wand question, "If I could wave a magic wand and accomplish one thing with your advertising, guaranteed, what would that one thing have to be?" Get a specific answer to that question and you've got a title for your proposal that will create anticipation and excitement on behalf of the client.

"How to Increase Sales of Certified Used Vehicles in a Challenging Environment"

"How to Own the Sedation Dentist Position in a Competitive Marketplace"

"Driving More Traffic to www.HurtatWorkNY.com"

Remember, we restate the title at the end of our Current Situation page.

I like to reference the Magic Wand question when I deliver the title to the client. I say, "We specifically titled this presentation, 'How to Increase Spinal Decompression Patients' because that's what **you told me** you wanted to do when I asked the Magic Wand question at the end of our last meeting..."

After you've invested your time in a good Time Out Call, make sure you let the client know you did your job and listened, and will deliver a solution to their needs. Make them take ownership of their words by using, "You told me..."

CHAPTER 27

THE COLUMBO SALES STRATEGY

ORIGINALLY PUBLISHED: 6/27/2011

2020 Perspective – Columbo. On MeTV. Check it out.

Peter Falk died last week. Peter Falk was the wonderful actor who portrayed one of television's iconic characters of the 1970's—Detective Columbo.

His subtle technique for uncovering the real information in his detective work always occurred as he was walking out the door. He would stop, turn around, and when the suspect's guard was down, he'd utter his catch phrase, "Ah, just one more thing..."

Inevitably, the "just one more thing" question was THE question that uncovered the critical piece of information.

This is how Sean McPheat of MTD Sales Training Specialists describes it:

Here's how to use the Columbo sales strategy...

Remember how Columbo would be questioning a suspect, the suspect would give him a reply that put him in the clear and then Columbo would agree with him and start to walk away. The camera would pan to the suspect's face, who would have that smug "I've got away with it look," and then Columbo would turn around, put his hand on his head and say, "Oh, by the way. There's just one more thing..."

And whammo, that question would rip open the suspect and expose their alibi.

The reason the Columbo Sales Strategy works is because

the Killer Question comes when the client's guard is down. "Ah, just one more thing..." catches the client when mentally they've decided that the meeting is over. Your notebook is put away, both you and the client are on your feet away from the meeting desk, and your "call" is officially over. That's when the real information can be exposed.

Senior Marketing Consultant, David Melville, refers to it as "The 46th Minute." David is a master at diagnosis, and he pays very close attention to the 46th minute. That's the time immediately after the official "Time Out Call" has ended, when clients are often more forthcoming.

I had a 46th Minute experience recently. I was meeting with a small casino in the Midwest. Our diagnosis all was good, I had wrapped up, but I still wasn't exactly sure about what my strategy might be. Then, as we were standing there sharing small talk before I left, the client said, "We're going to put a much greater emphasis on the late-night hours. We're keeping our kitchen open longer and we'll be the only casino in town with a late-night menu. Lots of people play more aggressively in the last couple hours of gaming because they're trying to catch up for their losses from the day."

Bingo! There's my strategy. Help them win the Late Night daypart. It was a total 46th Minute win.

Just because our notebooks are closed and we've officially ended our diagnosis, it doesn't mean we stop listening. Some of the best information comes when the client thinks the hard part is over... and, ah, just one more thing... don't be afraid to hold back a Killer Question to ask just before you walk out the door.

CHAPTER 28

THE COMPLEX SALE

ORIGINALLY PUBLISHED: 9/15/2011

2020 Perspective – I believe every sale today is a complex sale with multiple buying influences. Again, a product of the Great Recession and the evolution of business. Today, the opinion of the dental assistant matters as much as the practice manager and the dentist! Be respectful of all the buying influences. I absolutely love the bonus tip in this chapter...

We always tout getting in front of the "Economic Buyer." The Economic Buyer is that single person who can say "yes" when everyone else says "no." We're talking owners, CEO's, presidents of companies. It's imperative that in today's NEW economy, you're interacting at the highest level. We always say that in tougher economic times, advertising decisions are made higher up the ladder.

Now, here's the curve ball. In this NEW economy, while advertising decisions are being made higher up the ladder, there is greater influence by committee. In this NEW economy, economic buyers are including more opinions in the decision-making process. And, in fact, the economic buyer can actually be an "Economic Buying Committee."

Authors Miller and Heiman labeled it "the complex sale" years ago in their book, *Strategic Selling*. A complex sale is any sale that involves multiple decision-makers. Think about the last 10 sales you've made. How many involved more than one decision-maker? How many of those 10 had multiple players involved?

While we still strive to interact with the economic buyer in every instance, we need to be aware that there are usually multiple buying influences involved. Another truth is that the more decision-makers/influencers involved, the longer the buying process will take. Some research says that today it takes an average of 8 to 9 calls before a decision is reached, and the average number of people involved in the decision has ballooned to three to five, up from two decision-makers in decades past.

Here are 4 Tips for presenting to multiple decision-makers...

1. **Get Confirmation**. Before the presentation, get confirmation that all decision-making participants are attending and are committed to the entire presentation time. This may be like herding cats, but getting the group together is critical in your success.

2. **Watch for Clues**. During the presentation, pay attention to who's buying in and who's not. Try to determine who the thought leaders are, and once you win them over, use their clout to influence the others.

3. **Encourage Participation**. You need to uncover all feedback—positive and negative. Try to get the higher-ranking participants to open up. That will get others to participate once they see the top dogs engaged.

4. **Don't Slight Anyone**. Make sure all participants have a chance to speak. Ask specific questions of those who are reluctant to participate. Things like, "How will this decision affect your department?"

Bonus Tip: Here's a great multiple decision-maker technique I saw in a market recently. A smart AE had worked hard to corral all the buying influencers for the presentation meeting. The AE knew that getting the entire group to find a mutually agreeable time to discuss the specific issue of advertising was a monumental task. So, when they all came together for her presentation, she had them come to her conference room. It was set up with refreshments and treats, and all her AV needs were ready to go. She also knew it would be a long period of time before they ever got back together to discuss her proposal after she was done. So, she gave them the time at the conclusion of her presentation!

When the presentation was done and all the questions were answered, she said, "I know how hard it is to get everyone together, and I also know that you probably want to discuss my presentation among yourselves before you give me an answer. So, if there are no more questions for me, I'm going to leave you now. Please stay as long as you like in the conference room—it's reserved for you for the rest of the morning. I simply wanted to give you time to discuss my plan while it's fresh in your head." She even went as far as to have fresh coffee brought in at that time to really reinforce that the participants should stay.

Instead of concluding a group presentation and dismissing everyone, hoping they're so moved by your efforts that they'll quickly reconvene to come to a decision, go ahead and give them the time immediately following your presentation.

CHAPTER 29

COMMON SUCCESS STORY MISTAKES!

ORIGINALLY PUBLISHED: 5/19/2010

2020 Perspective – If you haven't figured it out yet, we're big believers in success stories at JDA. And, in today's challenging conditions, the currency of success stories just went up in value! However, they need to be the right stories, told properly.

In a recent training session with a media sales team, I shared the importance of including success stories. For those of you who listened to Jim Doyle's recent tele-seminar on reducing risk to increase sales, you heard Jim talk about including even more success stories than ever to knock down those walls of doubt. Nothing reduces risk more than powerful success stories. So, if you were including 1 or 2 stories in the past, maybe in today's climate you need 3, 4 or even 5 success stories, strategically placed throughout your presentation.

During my seminar, I had an AE say, "Tom, I do include success stories, but my clients don't seem to care about them. They act as if the stories aren't meaningful or aren't an indication of what could happen with their business. I just don't get that good of a reaction to success stories the way you and Jim think it happens…"

Interesting point. This AE thinks that clients aren't moved by success stories. Well, for 5 years I've watched clients listen intently as I've shared successes from around the country, so I'm convinced they work.

If your success stories aren't having the right affect, it's for one of two reasons:

1. They're not good stories (or the right stories)
2. Your delivery is wrong

Here are a few common success story mistakes...

You don't "own the material." I have witnessed time after time AE's poorly deliver powerful success stories because they don't own the story. When you don't own material, here's what happens...

- You stumble your way through the page
- You lose control because you become derailed
- You turn off the client because you look less professional
- You turn off the client because you're wasting their time (if you included a page but are not deliberate in presenting it, you're wasting the clients time)
- You're missing an opportunity to make an effective point

In the worst case ever, I saw an AE say, "Here's a success story from one of our clients. It's not my client, so I'm not sure of the details, but, well, you can read it later..." What?! The AE blew a chance to deliver an amazing story that beautifully displayed how a client concentrated their budget on her station and saw dramatic results.

Your Stories Miss the Point. I've seen many success stories that talk about how nice the AE is or how helpful the station is, but they say nothing about results. Success stories are about results—nothing else. Including a success story that only talks about how wonderful the partnership is, but never gives concrete results, is just like the advertiser whose commercial only talks about their customer service and never gives a strong offer or call to action.

No Passion in Delivery. An amazing success story

needs to be delivered with passion. If your media outlet helped a client increase sales by 12% in a down economy, you have to be able to get excited about delivering that message! I have a great success story about an OB/GYN that was up 5% in newborn deliveries last year. I can tell that story with incredible passion because the deliveries in the market overall were down 8%! That's a 13% swing! Passion in your delivery increases the level of excitement and believability in your presentation.

They're the Wrong Stories. I recently reviewed a proposal that was for a senior living facility. Included in the proposal was a success story for a bridal shop that had used the station and had a successful prom dress season. Why would you tell a senior living facility a prom dress success story? If I was the senior living facility buyer, I'd question how one media outlet could be right for such diverse audiences.

Or, the other big "wrong story" mistake is when AE's tell small direct clients success stories from the market's biggest advertisers. Don't tell a plumber with a tiny budget how well your station works for the biggest car dealership in town. He can't relate to that. Tell the plumber about the little retailer who can only afford to run one week a month but always gets a traffic increase. Tell the plumber about the roofing company who has consistently used weekends to drive phone calls on Monday. Tell stories that the client can relate to.

Our rule of thumb is this; tell out-of-market in-category stories, tell in-market out-of-category success stories. You don't want to tell one car dealer how well you are doing for their biggest competitor in town. In fact, many business owners have egos that make them say, "I would never do what that guy does". And, I'll never forget the time I was working in a hyphenated market and told a success story to a car dealer in "Market A" from a car dealer in "Market B". We thought we were safe in telling the story until the end of the meeting when the car dealer said, "I would stop telling that car dealer success story. He just called me yesterday and asked me to buy his dealership because he's doing so poorly." Ouch!

CHAPTER 30

WHAT ONE THING WOULD YOU CHANGE?

ORIGINALLY PUBLISHED: 7/23/2012

2020 Perspective – This is the best response to the "let me think about it" objection I've ever discovered.

You've just completed your presentation. You're hoping for a signature, a handshake, something that says this deal is moving forward. Then you hear this, "I like it, but I'm not quite ready to sign off right now" or "Let me take this back to my manager/boss/wife and we'll get back to you" or "I never sign anything right away. Let me sleep on it. I promise I'll get back to you soon."

Has that ever happened to you? If you've been selling for any length of time, it has! What do you do? Most of us simply get a commitment like, "Can I get back with you in a few days?" and hope for the best. Some of us will ask, "Can I present this to any other decision-maker?" and hope to win all decision-makers over in another presentation round.

Well, here's a great question to ask at that point of stall…

"Now that you've seen my entire proposal, what one thing would you change about it?" This question is a real game-changer! Please note, the question is NOT, "Would you change anything?" it's "What ONE THING would you change?" It gets right to the heart of any real future objection… if there is one.

The problem with "would you change anything" is it allows the prospect to deliver a closed-ended answer: yes or no. The question, "What one thing would you change about it?" must lead to a discussion. I would also press the prospect for a change. First of all, it would be shocking if there was absolutely nothing at all that needed to be changed. Almost all proposals have some sort of change—in budget, start date, schedule strategy—something usually gets tweaked.

If the prospect really insists that NOTHING needs to be changed, when stall time comes around, you can remind them that there was nothing to change—so what are we waiting for?

"Now that you've seen my entire proposal, what one thing would you change about it?" allows you the opportunity to immediately address the biggest objection, be it price, strategy, time-frame, whatever... Try it at the conclusion of your next presentation and see what happens!

CHAPTER 31

SHHHHHH!

ORIGINALLY PUBLISHED: 9/20/2008

2020 Perspective – I learned very early on in my consulting career to embrace silence. At first it was simply a "fake it 'til you make it" necessity. Today, I enjoy pushing the silence envelope. I find I get some of my best information after a long pause. It's not surprising that I wrote this article in September of 2008, at the apex of the collapse!

"Silence is a fence around wisdom." -German Proverb

I had just asked the client to describe his ideal customer. He sat back and pondered the question with a long pause. You could sense the wheels turning in his head as he prepared to describe the absolute prime candidate he would love to see walk through the door. I sat at the ready, pen in hand, anxiously waiting to capture his next words...

All of a sudden, the AE next to me starts blurting out descriptions on behalf of the client.

"Silence please!" I thought to myself. "Let's hear from the client, not you!"

A few moments later I was uncovering growth opportunities moving forward. I had been engaged in a strong Time Out Call for a good half-hour and was really digging deep. I took a long pause to craft my next question, but before I could end the silence, the AE jumps in with a completely unrelated question. It was a panic question that was thrown out just to end the silence.

Finally, we got to the budget questions. I was successful in getting actual figures for various media. Then I asked, "So, in all of your advertising and marketing, how much will you invest total in 2008?" The client chuckled uncomfortably and replied, "Too much." I wanted more, so I sat tight, completely locked on the client. He knew that answer wasn't going to be good enough for me. It was a powerful moment, only to be interrupted by the AE jumping in to let the client off the hook!

It was obvious to me, this AE feared silence.

Silence in selling is a very powerful skill. It can be used for emphasis, to heighten the dramatic effect, even to create tension. Silence in the Time Out Call can signal intense concentration, understanding, even respect. I was earning my respect as a professional by not accepting a brush-off answer for a critical question. We're not there to simply launch softballs to our clients, not if we really want to help them. Sometimes, we need to offer silence to give our clients the opportunity to successfully answer a question.

I find that those people who fear silence are typically the same people who feel the need to show how smart they are by adding unnecessary information. Think of the saying, "The strong, silent type." What image does that conjure in your head? Thoughtful. Powerful. Respected. Deliberate. Intelligent. Determined. All qualities you want to exude during your Time Out Call.

Next time you feel compelled to end a silence, give pause. Don't fear silence. Master it and use it for the powerful tool it can be.

In the words of Dr. Evil, "Zip it!"

SECTION 2:

ADVERTISING IN CHALLENGING CONDITIONS

CHAPTER 32

MY 2 DEFAULT VALUE PROPOSITIONS

ORIGINALLY PUBLISHED: 11/18/2009

2020 Perspective – I think these two value propositions are probably even more important today! In tough times, everyone wants value. And, I continue to see businesses win by claiming the speed position in their category. A "Call us this morning, we will see you TODAY!" message run on Monday mornings is a homerun for tons of categories. Legal, dentist, HVAC, chiropractor, you name it... it never fails.

I think the biggest problem with most local, direct businesses is that they have no demonstrable unique value proposition. When it comes right down to it, much of the time the local advertiser can't come up with a good, compelling reason that a prospect should choose them over their competitor. That's a sad statement to make.

Far and away, the most common answer I get to the question, "Why should I come see you vs. your competition?" is "It's our service!"

This is not a "service is not a differentiator" article. I've written about that many times.

When I have to really press a client for their Value Proposition, I can usually default to one of two things:

- Price
- Speed

If the client can't come up with their own USP, I try one of these two value propositions. Think about it... if the business owner can't come up with a single differentiator, then his product better be cheaper than everyone else's, or I'd better be able to get it faster than any other business can deliver.

Marketing Experiments Journal identifies characteristics of a strong value proposition this way:

- You must differentiate your offer from a competitor's offer
- You may match the competition on every dimension of value *except one*
- You need to excel in at least one element of value
- In this way you become the Best Choice

Here are some ways to present the PRICE value proposition:

- Lower overhead
- Factory direct
- Better buying power

These are some rational ways to deliver a price message. CAUTION: I'm not saying these are the end-all. We certainly know that rational doesn't always work! But these are great starting points to help form a lower price USP.

Here are some ways to present the SPEED value proposition:

- In stock inventory for immediate delivery
- Larger service fleet
- 24-hour emergency service

A claim of speed, backed up by a guarantee, is a great combination. Think of the plumber who says, "On time or you don't pay a dime!"

When you're stuck trying to help a local advertiser develop a strong USP, consider the two default value propositions—price and speed—and see if there's a demonstrable way to incorporate either of them into a good, strong Unique Selling Proposition.

CHAPTER 33

THE CONFUSION OF CHOICES

ORIGINALLY PUBLISHED: 1/13/2008

2020 Perspective – A confused mind will never buy.

Recently, I met with a financial planner to discuss some investment options. He sat at my kitchen table and presented various strategies. In this arena, he's the expert and I am definitely not! After exploring several options, I asked for his recommendation. This is where his sales efforts fell apart. He circled 3 or 4 options and told me, "They're all good. Any one of them would work for you."

That was NOT the answer I was looking for. I wanted a definitive, singular selection with a firm, "Based on your needs, this is clearly the choice for you."

Choices and selection are a good thing... if you're shopping for sofas. But when you're trying to get an expert recommendation, most buyers want to hear from a confident professional.

When it comes to presenting your recommended solution, don't provide choices. In the past, you may have offered two, maybe even three, options for your client to choose—a kind of good, better, best selection. The traditional school of thought was that the client would pick the middle option. Rather than let the client have control, based on the information you discovered in a diagnosis call, you should present *one* recommendation. You are the expert when it comes to making your station work for your clients. Be firm, take control, and deliver your best recommendation.

Be careful not to waffle, either. It's one thing to be flexible to accommodate a client, it's another to lose control and waffle. Have rationale and reason for your strategy, so that when your client challenges you, you're able to respond confidently. For example, if a client questions the validity of your morning news in the strategy, be prepared to stand by your recommendation with your reasons for including it: "Our morning news delivers a strong female head-of-household audience that matches perfectly with your core customer, and these are regular viewers we can reach with high frequency."

I've witnessed many account executives who are quick to bail from their recommended plan at any sign of client pushback. This sends the message that you don't know your product as well as your client. When you say, "We can do whatever you want," you're not being accommodating as much as you're saying, "I'm not really sure what will work for you—you know as much as I do..."

Put your recommended strategy together with reason and rationale. Don't offer choices. Be confident and firm when delivering the schedule you recommend. You're the expert on helping clients earn results with your station.

CHAPTER 34

MANAGE THE EXPECTATIONS

ORIGINALLY PUBLISHED: 3/28/2010

2020 Perspective – *You must set specific expectations and metrics in advance of the campaign. Today, with our access to digital metrics, it's easier than ever to measure. Just make sure you're measuring the right thing and that the client agrees it's the right thing to measure!*

I was meeting with three dentists. Their practice had been advertising for almost a year.

"Is it working, Dr. Smith?" I asked.

"I can't say that I've seen any new patients directly from the television advertising" he replied.

"Interesting. Dr. Klein, do you think it's working?"

"I really have no idea," he answered.

"How about you Dr. Lin, do you think the television advertising is working?" I asked the last doctor.

Dr. Lin said, "Since we began the campaign, I'm up double digits. Last month, I set our office record for the most new patients seen in one month and I'll break that record at the end of this month. I've done $60,000 in revenue in the procedure we're promoting." He turned to his partners and said, "I don't know how you're tracking, but there's no doubt in my mind that it's working."

This is a real scenario that happened recently. After nearly a year of advertising, 2 of the 3 dentists in the practice have no idea whether the advertising is working, yet the third dentist is reaping tremendous benefits. What's going on here? Lack of communication, lack of accountability, lack of interest.

Then, there was the bowling alley lady. Six months ago, we recommended she focus her entire message on birthday parties. This is a good point of entry, as birthday parties are profitable and she had capacity to do more. Six months into the campaign, she's unhappy. Birthday parties are up, overall bowling business is up, but customers aren't asking for the specific (and by the way, most expensive) birthday party package being promoted. So, she's unhappy, yet birthday parties are up and overall business is up!

What do these two case studies have in common? They're both success stories where the client doesn't even know they're a success story! We failed to identify, in advance, the metrics to measure to determine success.

We need to make sure we're asking, "What has to happen in order for you to deem this a success?" Along with that question, we need to help the clients understand how they're going to measure results.

In the bowling alley case, we all assumed that if birthday parties were up and overall business was up, then the advertising would be deemed successful. However, in the client's mind, all that mattered was increasing sales of the specific birthday party package she was advertising.

In the dentist's case, you clearly have two dentists who are not tracking well and one who has embraced the program and is tracking the results. What a shame that nearly a year into a program that's clearly delivering results, two of the three partners don't even know that it's working.

And, how many times have we run campaigns where the client says the website is the call to action and then we go back and hear, "It didn't work, nobody called." Had we asked, "What has to happen?" and discovered it was phone calls that were the goal, then we would have changed the call to action.

This is a reminder to all Achievers to clearly identify what has to happen in order for the campaign to be deemed a success in the mind of the advertiser.

CHAPTER 35

IT'S TOUGH OUT THERE, IT'S TIME TO BE MORE CREATIVE!

ORIGINALLY PUBLISHED: 4/17/2008

2020 Perspective – Okay, I'm a stickler for creative. I truly believe the main reason our campaigns fail is the message. Heck, I'm the guy who wrote Branding is OUT, Results are IN! In challenging conditions, strong creative becomes even more important. Here are some things to consider:

- *On the "need to want" scale, what is your advertiser selling? Emergency HVAC repair? A need. Or outdoor kitchens? A want. Is your client's product or service an essential, a treat, a postponable or an expendable? The type of purchase matters.*

- *Who's the target for the purchase, and what is their state of mind right now? Are they a "slam-on-the-brakes, shut down all spending, fearful" consumer? Are they an "in pain but able to make a cautious purchase" buyer? Are they a "live for today, deal with it later" buyer? Who will be making the purchase?*

- *In tough times, focus on value, packaging, reward loyalty, defer payments, take advantage of low interest rates.*

- *Personally, I'm not into the "feel good, we're here for you" messaging for most local advertisers. Leave that up to Ford and Chevy. Plus, the shelf life on that is short. As soon as we start peeking our heads out again, you're going to have a nation of weary consumers who want value—in everything.*

There's no question it's getting tougher and tougher on the streets these days. Clients are nervous, corporate is nervous, your manager is nervous. So, now more than ever, is NOT the time to roll up into a ball of conservatism, particularly with your creative ideas.

Now is the time to stretch your creative comfort zone. Break out of those boundaries you've imposed and think about creative ideas that you might normally have stifled.

Why do I write this? Because lately, I've experienced some pushback on creative ideas from account executives. I've heard things like, "That's not what my client is looking for," and "That's not the type of commercial our station produces." Guess what? Your client is looking for creative ideas that will get them noticed. And, trust me, you've got talent in your production departments, along with a lot of really cool expensive equipment that's dying to get used!

I remember a great line a production director once told me when I was sweating the details during production. He said, "Making commercials is like making ice cream cones. Sometimes they lean to the right, sometimes they lean to the left, sometimes they're just right—but they all taste good!" That was back in the day when you could put just about anything on and get results.

Times are different now. The consumer faces much more clutter and noise in their daily life. And, in these challenging economic times, it's more important than ever to stand out from the competition.

I was recently working with an MRI facility. We presented them with a unique creative idea that was singularly focused on owning the position of speed in her category. They do same-day appointments and guaranteed 24-hour turnaround on results. We showed a charging thoroughbred to hammer home

101

the speed claim (we were in the middle of horse country). Never did we suggest pictures of the CAT scan machine or any docs wearing lab coats. The client loved the idea. Unfortunately, the client had just signed an annual with a competing station and was waiting for their creative concept. I told them that it was my guess that the other station would bring them a script that used words like "caring professionals" and showed images of big machines being operated by thoughtful medical staff. Very cliché.

I suggested that if they could remove their logo from the commercial and slap on the logo of their competitor and the commercial would work for them, then it was time to go back to the drawing board! You haven't successfully communicated any point of difference.

The client loved our creative idea and is considering switching the annual.

When you find yourself writing advertising blah, blah... stop! Force yourself to push your creative comfort zone. It's easy to write cliché commercials. Creativity may take a little more time and effort, but the results are worth it. Involve your production department, and if they come up with a unique (maybe even goofy) idea, think twice before you shoot it down. You don't want to be the person in the AFLAC boardroom who said, "A duck! Are you kidding me!?"

CHAPTER 36

IS IT TIME TO ADVERTISE PRICE?

ORIGINALLY PUBLISHED: 8/2/2008

2020 Perspective – Of course, not every business is intended to be the low-price leader. My message here is that even with luxury, we still want to know "how much does it cost?" Heck, every luxury brand of automobile advertises a monthly payment!

More than ever in the past six months, I've homed in on pricing during my diagnosis calls. I start with the perception question by asking, "If I asked 100 people around town, "What do you think of when you hear the name (insert business name here), what would they tell me?" After the client says things like great service, good people, and the typical blah, blah, I'll ask, "What about pricing?"

When I hear the client respond, "Some people might consider us pricey," I really start to dig deeper. What I find is that most upscale or higher end businesses—the ones the market considers pricey—shy away from advertising price. I certainly understand that when you're not the low-price leader in a market, price may not be the way to bring your message to the market.

However, in today's economic climate, I now believe that price matters at all levels. Let me share a recent exchange I had with a "pricey" business...

I met with the owner of a high-end lighting store, let's call them Tiffany Lighting and Electric. They had never advertised price in any of their television advertising. The owner told me, "I can't compete, nor do I want to, with the prices that the big-box stores advertise." We were discussing his Memorial Day sale. He showed me the creative he had written. After the regular blah, blah of "64 years of serving the _____ market...," he got to the offer—"save up to 70% on all ceiling fans."

He asked me to red pen his creative. The first thing I did was eliminate the blah, blah (when buying a new ceiling fan, does anybody care that the store has been in business for 64 years!). Then, I asked him what he thought was the most popular ceiling fan he had, and to give me the sale price on it. I then added to the 70%-off offer by including this one fan, priced at $149.

He told me he couldn't do that because everyone knows you can go to Home Depot and buy a ceiling fan for $49.

I told him that while the consumer could go to Home Depot and buy something for a lot less, they don't **aspire** to do so! They do aspire to come to the beautiful Tiffany Lighting and Electric. I said, "What does the lady of the house want to answer when a guest asks where she got her beautiful new ceiling fan—Home Depot or Tiffany Lighting?"

When the perceived "pricey" store only advertises a percentage off, the consumer has no frame of reference. All they know is they think they probably can't afford to shop that store, so 40%, 50%, even 70% off means nothing!

Here's the killer line to use with the client who fights you on including price. Just say:

"Doesn't it bother you that today, someone will buy the type of product you sell, for the amount that you sell it for, and you never got a shot at them because they think they couldn't afford you!"

I have used this line with the electric and lighting store (doesn't it bother you that today, someone in this town is going to buy a ceiling fan for $149 and they never came here because they didn't think they could afford you!).

I've used it with high-end kitchen remodelers (doesn't it bother you that today, someone in this town is going to spend $20,000 on a kitchen remodel and you never got a shot at them because they didn't even know they could afford to come here).

I've used it with carpet stores, replacement windows, anything where the client is perceived as pricey (especially when competing with a big-box).

Today, when every consumer is budget conscious, and every advertiser is trying harder and harder to earn results, I would seriously consider including price, especially when working with the perceived "pricey" client.

If the perceived myth is that the client is pricey, the best way to blow up that myth is with price-point advertising.

CHAPTER 37

MORE THOUGHTS ON UPSCALE ADVERTISERS

ORIGINALLY PUBLISHED: 7/19/2010

2020 Perspective – *Frankly, I don't think the "even upscale buyers want value" shift of the Great Recession ever went away. And, I think it will become even more important post-Coronavirus Crisis.*

Last week, we talked a lot about dealing with advertisers who refuse to mention price. Typically, these are advertisers who are considered "upscale" in their category. They're the lighting store that can't compete with the big-box store competition, the furniture store that takes the upscale position against the Ashley store in the market or the high-end home remodeler/pool builder/landscaper, etc.

As we stated in last week's article, in healthy economic conditions, the upscale position is a strong position to hold, and it's not always about advertising price. But, when times are tough, even upscalers need to take a look at how they're positioning themselves in a market.

Consider this information from a recent *USA Today* article:

- Nearly three in four wealthy women say they'll only purchase luxuries if they can get a good deal, reports a recent survey by AgencySacks,
- Luxury spending slid 7.8% last year to $10.1 billion, says Spending Pulse, a consumer spending monitor from MasterCard. It's bounced back up for the first 5

months of 2010, but even affluent customers continue to seek out discounts, bargains and sales. In a recent MasterCard poll, some 64% of all consumers said they were shopping sales.

Upscale brands from Coach to Sony are launching products with lower price points aimed at delivering luxury at a perceived bargain. "A few years ago, you'd just market access to the affluent. Now, you need to market access—along with a discount," says MasterCard's Tim Murphy.

I wouldn't suggest local businesses abandon the "upscale" position if they've earned it over the years. I would, however, suggest they tweak their approach to marketing and figure ways to appeal to a buyer's sense of a deal.

"A lot of people feel like chumps if they pay full price," says Gilt.com CEO, Susan Lyne. "When you get a deal on a luxury item, it makes you feel smart."

As consumers, we all want to feel smart.

CHAPTER 38

FEAR SELLS IN 2009

ORIGINALLY PUBLISHED: 12/21/2008

2020 Perspective – _This chapter is the epitome of Recession Lessons! I wrote this article in December of 2008. We were a mere 45 days into the Great Recession. It was as tough as I've ever experienced leading into a new year, and advertisers were panicked. So were consumers. Just like it is today. Fear sells in 2020._

In the new book _Buy-ology, Truth and Lies About Why We Buy_, author Martin Lindstrom says that _fear sells_. He cites the infamous "Daisy" ad from 1964 for then presidential candidate Lyndon Johnson, in which a young girl is seen frolicking with a daisy as a nuclear explosion detonates.

He says, "...Johnson's 'Daisy' ad helped to ensure victory in 1964 by playing to the fear of nuclear war. Despite widespread cries that political advertising emphasizes 'optimism,' 'hope,' 'building up, not tearing down' and so on, **fear works. It's what our brains remember."**

We can use this knowledge to help our clients get better advertising results, especially in the current economic conditions. In today's climate, consumers are paralyzed. I think as consumers, we are far more concerned today with **not making a mistake** than we are with **doing the right thing.** I may need a new roof on my house, it may be the right thing to do, but my fear is preventing me from pulling the trigger on that investment right now. Purchases are being put on hold out of fear.

When you're writing copy or helping your client determine an action-provoking offer, try to think how the consumer thinks, and see if you can play to their emotion of fear. For example, in today's climate, instead of saying, "save $500," I contend it's better to advertise something like this: "Don't make a $500 mistake!"

A simple repositioning of the very same offer could deliver much greater results.

I love the used car dealer who advertises, "Go to our website to learn 'The 5 Things New Car Dealers Don't Want You Know!' This totally plays on the consumer's fear that they're being taken advantage of by new car dealers.

TV news departments have been using this type of technique for years. Which do you think is a more powerful promo:

Coming up, find out why a safe kitchen is a happy kitchen...

Or

Coming up, find out what's in your kitchen that could kill you!

Fear sells.

So, the next time you start writing an ad that says new windows could **save** you hundreds, consider instead a simple twist and say, "Your current windows are **costing** you hundreds..."

CHAPTER 39

RECONSIDER THE OFFER

ORIGINALLY PUBLISHED: 3/1/2009

2020 Perspective – The stakes just got higher!

It's time to seriously reconsider the offers you make in your creative. Denny's Super Bowl offer has raised the bar for everyone. FREE. No strings attached. Just come in. Now that was an offer!

Today, I grabbed my Sunday paper (I know, some of us still do that) and stickered on the top of the front page was an ad for a local pizzeria. First of all, how bad is it when the paper is selling stickers that cover the headlines on the front of the Sunday paper? That's like starting the six o'clock news with your anchor wearing a hat that says, "Eat at Joe's." But things are tough, so the paper has found another revenue generator— a front-page sticker—okay. The real tragedy was the offer: "bring in this sticker and get 10% off your order." Ten percent? Ten measly percent?!? You go through the trouble of making stickers to put on the front page of the newspaper and then you offer a 10% discount on your pizza? Who's going to change their pizza eating habits for 10% off? It ain't gonna work. Then, we have another business that will be saying advertising doesn't work... or at least newspaper advertising doesn't.

Reconsider the offer!

Folks, the stakes are higher, way higher. I know it's a catch-22 for your advertisers, just when their business is at its worst is when we have to tell them to give better offers.

But that's the skin it takes to get in the game. Remember a few weeks ago when we dissected the Denny's Super Bowl promotion? We said that it never would have generated the same buzz if the offer had been a $.99 breakfast, or a Buy One, Get One.

As you prepare more campaigns for local direct advertisers, an outstanding offer is one of the critical elements in the success formula. You need to push your clients to create something motivating, something tangible. And, you need to help them understand what works and what doesn't. For example, it's better to say, "Buy four replacement windows, get the 5th FREE!" than it is to say, "Save 20% on replacement windows right now." It's the same offer, but one clearly sounds better—FREE.

Now, let's take this lesson one step further. Last week, I spent time in a market presenting strategies and ideas to advertisers. As a closing tool, we offered a 20% bonus structure if the client would sign that week. No matter how much or how long you bought, we'd bonus you back 20%! Guess what? It wasn't enough. Today, in this challenging climate, 20% doesn't get advertisers excited.

I'm all for rate integrity, etc., but the bar has been raised, for our clients and for us. Take those unused national avails and put them to work for your local advertisers. Identify those who still have budgets to spend and bring them your version of the Denny's Deal! Create an offer to which they can't say "no." All budgets are up for grabs these days. Be bold in asking, be bold in giving.

As John Jantsch says in his book *Duct Tape Marketing*, "Create an astonishing offer, one that makes you nervous—and that's the point. If you could create and communicate an offer that nobody in your industry would even consider, you would automatically have two very powerful things going for you: a core marketing message that would differentiate you from your competition, and a forced focus on delivering excellence and winning loyal, repeat customers. An astonishing offer turns heads, an astonishing offer generates buzz, an astonishing offer creates a mission."

Now, reconsider the offer, and make it astonishing!

CHAPTER 40

PICK A PROBLEM

ORIGINALLY PUBLISHED: 10/13/2011

2020 Perspective – *"What's your biggest priority for the next six months?" This question just became more important. When times are tough, we may need to pivot and focus on the single biggest priority of the day.*

Recently, an account executive sent me a proposal to review. The title read, "Helping Smith Motors Dramatically Increase New Car Sales, Drive Traffic to the Used Lot, and Grow Service Department Revenue."

My spidey-sense tingled. "I smell danger!" I thought.

Have you ever written a title like that? Many of us have. When we met with Smith Motors, Mr. Smith told us he'd like to sell more new cars. Of course, he also told us he'd like to see more used traffic, and, by the way, he could always use more service department business. So, in our desire to please Mr. Smith, we wrap all of his wishes into one title, one proposal, and probably one ill-conceived solution to accomplish all of this.

Would we be better served, would Mr. Smith be better served, if we only focused on one of his issues—his most immediate and compelling issue?

We tell our clients they should have a singular focus. We need to heed that advice, as well. For example, just because the real estate company says they'd like to increase both buyers and sellers, doesn't mean we should try to accomplish both, especially in the same campaign. In fact, in real estate they say, "list to last." When you get right down to it, advertising for listings is a much smarter strategy than "Driving Buyers AND Sellers to Jones Real Estate."

Here's a simple question I ask when a client or prospect has dumped multiple problems (or opportunities) in my lap. I know I can't accomplish everything or solve all of his issues, especially in one proposal or campaign strategy, so I simply ask, "Of everything we just talked about, what is your biggest priority for the next 6 months?" This question helps me focus on the ONE THING that is the biggest immediate priority, and in fact, that's what the client wants and needs—a good solution to address their biggest immediate priority.

For example, I'd ask Mr. Smith of Smith Motors, "Of all the things we just discussed—new car sales, used lot traffic, service—what's your biggest priority for the next six months?" When Mr. Smith says, "Well, we really need to continue to focus on used sales, that's our bread and butter," we'd return with a proposal titled, "How to Increase Traffic to the Used Lot and Drive Sales of Pre-Owned."

Don't feel compelled to address every problem, opportunity, desire, wish, that is uncovered in your diagnosis call. Just because the client mentions in passing that they'd like to build a few more patios to go with the vinyl decks they build, (which is really their bread and butter) doesn't mean we need to include patios in the proposal.

The more singular and specific your title is:
- The more believable your solution becomes
- The more focused the client becomes
- The more excited the client becomes to accomplish their BIGGEST immediate priority
- The greater your closing percentage!

And, when you've identified the right singular focus, clients rarely ask about secondary and tertiary concerns, even if they seemed to dwell on them in the diagnosis call.

So, the next time the symphony tells you they want to increase single performance ticket sales, grow more season ticket holders, and increase corporate donations, ask which is the single biggest priority for the next six months. Or, "If I could make one of those things happen, which would be most important?"

CHAPTER 41

IT'S NOT JUST ABOUT ASKING THE QUESTIONS

ORIGINALLY PUBLISHED: 3/1/2010

2020 Perspective – A decade after I wrote this article, I still see it happening all the time—account executives who take out our diagnosis questions and faithfully ask all the questions, but it's clear they didn't listen to the answers. They simply asked and recorded, asked and recorded, asked and recorded. My colleague, Pat Norris, calls them "bobblehead AE's." They simply nod and write down the answer with zero thought as to what it means. Now is the time to listen carefully and understand what's being said, so you can customize the right strategy.

Last week, I was sent Time Out Call notes from an AE who called on a local flooring company. He wanted me to review his notes and see if I could help him come up with a strategy. As I reviewed the notes, it became apparent that the AE had asked all the questions, but what really came to the surface was that the AE either didn't listen to the answers or didn't know what to do with the information.

For example, the AE had asked the client about the competitive landscape, yet here's what he sent me:

Q. *Who are your biggest competitors?*

A. J & M Flooring and Carpet One

Q. *What are their biggest strengths?*

A. They don't have any

Q. *What are their biggest weaknesses?*

A. Don't know

Seriously, you can't allow the client to get away with this! You can't simply ask the questions and write down whatever the client says with no clarification, follow-up or challenge. You can't truly believe that the entire competitive landscape in the flooring category has no competitive strengths.

And then the AE shares this:

Q. *One a scale of 1 to 10, what is most important to your customer?*

A. Location: 9
Price: 6
Selection: 7
Service: 10
Quality: 7

Q. *How are you perceived in the market?*

A. Too expensive

Well, if the store is perceived as too expensive, shouldn't "price" outrank everything else on "what is important to the customer"?

My point is that the Time Out Call is not just a mindless exercise of asking questions and recording answers. If it were that easy, we'd create an online form and simply email the client a link and tell them to fill out the form at their convenience. But it's not that simple. The Time Out Call is a mental give-and-take with a client. It's your thought-provoking exercise to put the pieces of the puzzle together. When things don't make sense, you need to ask follow-ups, dig deeper, and investigate.

Ask any Jim Doyle & Associates Senior Marketing Consultant and they will tell you that the most exhausting week we have is when we spend 5 days performing Time Out Call after Time Out Call. It's because each Time Out Call is 45-minutes-plus of intense concentration. It's more than just asking the questions. It's listening and understanding what to do with the information.

CHAPTER 42

THE LAST DOLLAR IN IS THE BEST DOLLAR SPENT

ORIGINALLY PUBLISHED: 4/19/2009

2020 Perspective – Still true. The last dollar in is the best dollar spent. In challenging conditions, when advertisers are cutting back, the correct strategy is to eliminate "glasses," not simply reduce each one.

When we're presenting our recommendations and proposals to our clients, there is a tremendous amount of information being shared. Think of everything that's being introduced to the client. We've got audience A's and Z's, we've got singular messaging, there are glasses overflowing on the table, and that's all on one PowerPoint slide! That's an awful lot for our clients to take in.

But, there is one concept that needs to be shared each and every time you're presenting your proposal. It's *"the last dollar in is the best dollar spent."* We share this concept during our discussion of concentration. The concept of *last dollar in is the best dollar spent* is such an important element to successful advertising, that it's worthy of some special consideration. Let's bring a little more clarity to this important idea.

As we're sharing the "Principle of the Glasses," we tell the client to overflow the glass to achieve maximum impact—to gain the high, high frequency we're looking for. It's at this point that I'll tell the client, "We like to say that *the last dollar in is the best dollar spent.*" Then, I'll oftentimes repeat the line, *"The last dollar in is the best dollar spent,"* and let the concept settle in with the client. Next, I'll say something like, "This is the momentum of advertising working for you. Advertising builds (I demonstrate by putting my hands one on top of the other and building upward), so that each dollar in the glass takes advantage of the one spent before it—every new dollar that goes in becomes more and more effective. So, again, the *last dollar in is the best dollar spent.*"

I believe the *last dollar in* concept is so important that I've created another little analogy to help our clients understand. Here's how I say it...

"I was thinking about this last dollar in concept one day while I was on the treadmill. I thought, this concept is... just like being on a treadmill! Say you decided to do 30 minutes on the treadmill. Near the end of your 29th minute you think, *wow what a good workout. But, if I do just 5 more minutes, that would be the best 5 minutes spent on the treadmill. And if I did 5 minutes after that, that would be even better.* The last minute on is the best minute on, the last dollar in, is the best dollar in."

Share this analogy with anyone who has done any sort of cardio training and they'll really get it.

The last dollar in concept really drives home the Principle of the Glasses. I urge you to make sure you're giving this concept it's full consideration in your presentations. If you initially spend the time to solidify this concept, you can refer to it often in future discussions, most notably, when things are going so well for the client that you've helped create additional advertising budget. At that point, when the client asks you where you would spend it, you can say, "Right here with me because *the last dollar in is the best dollar spent!*"

119

SECTION 3:

A BETTER YOU

CHAPTER 43

THE FARMER AND THE TRACTOR SALESMAN...

ORIGINALLY PUBLISHED: 8/9/2008

2020 Perspective – *I love this story! Lesson: in tough times, people will use any excuse to not meet with you. It's better to qualify sooner rather than later.*

Years ago, when I was a young, impressionable media account executive, a sales manager told me the story about the farmer who refused to meet with the tractor salesman. The story delivers a powerful message and is worth sharing in today's economic climate. It goes like this...

One day, the new tractor salesman approaches the farmer in the field and says to the farmer, "I see your tractor is looking a little old. I sure would like to take a few minutes and show you our new line of equipment."

The farmer replies, "Well, I'd really like to see what you got, but now is not a good time. You see, my dog is dying."

"Oh, I'm really sorry to hear that," replies the tractor salesman. "I'll come see you on my next visit to the area."

About a month goes by and the tractor salesman returns to the area and visits the farmer. "I see you're still on top of that old tractor. I'd really like to show you our new line," he says.

"And I'd really like to see what you got, but not today. My dog is dying," replies the farmer.

"Oh, okay," says the puzzled tractor salesman. "I'll come see you next time around."

Another month goes by and the tractor salesman is back

to see the farmer. "That old tractor of yours is looking pretty rough," he says. "I have some real exciting new products to show you."

"Well, I am sure it's exciting, but now is not a good time because my dog is dying," replies the farmer.

At this point, the tractor salesman is completely frustrated. "Sir, with all due respect, I fail to see how the fact that your dog is dying prevents you from looking at my new product."

To which the farmer replies, "Son, when I ain't buyin', one excuse is as good as the next!"

When I was first told this story as a very fresh account executive, I didn't quite get it. Then, as I spent months on the street and encountered many "farmers," it started to make real sense to me. As a manager, I've shared this story with every new AE (and probably all of the veterans as well!) whom I've managed. When AE's would come back to the office with all the excuses in the book as to why they couldn't get the appointment or close the proposal after the third try, I'd just look at them and say, "His dog is dying."

In today's economic climate, there are a lot of "dogs dying." Clients and prospects will use any excuse to put off meeting with media reps. It's our job to create enough perceived value in our meeting or make the decision to cut and run. When you hear a "dog is dying" excuse—the objection that just doesn't make any sense or really isn't a legitimate reason to not proceed—it's better to call it out sooner, rather than later, to make sure you're spending your time in front of the right clients and prospects.

CHAPTER 44

3 WAYS TO REDUCE RISK

ORIGINALLY PUBLISHED: 10/14/2009

2020 Perspective – Jim Doyle says, "Selling is nothing more than the process of reducing risk. If there were no risk at all, they'd always say yes…" In challenging conditions, the need to reduce risk goes up dramatically.

What risk is swirling around in the mind of the potential advertiser? It's things like:
- Are you the right advertising vehicle?
- Will I see a return on my advertising dollar?
- Is the message correct?
- Can I measure it?
- If I do this, do I need to do anything else?
- Is it too much?
- Is it not enough?
- Can I afford to do it?
- Can I afford to not do it?

In the Doyle organization, we believe that selling is a process of reducing risk. The more you can reduce risk in the mind of the buyer, the greater your chances of making a sale and making a partner.

Here are three ways you can help reduce risk in the mind of the potential advertiser.

1. **Success Stories!** The very best way to reduce risk is to share success stories. Nothing makes a client feel better about using your advertising vehicle than stories

about other businesses like theirs that are seeing results with you. We preach that "Facts tell, stories sell." A few good, results-proving success stories go much further with a skittish prospect than ratings, CPP's and competitive bashing. And, in today's environment, we're increasing the number of success stories we share. In the past, we'd use one or two to demonstrate the strength of our plans and ideas. Now, we're including three, four, sometimes five success stories to really hammer home the point. And you want to choose success stories that the client can relate to. It's better to show a plumber prospect a success story from a replacement windows company or carpet cleaning business that spends in the same neighborhood of what you're asking, than showing them a success story from the local car dealership that regularly spends far more money and uses many other advertising outlets.

2. **ROI Demonstration.** After success stories, the next best way to reduce risk is to be able to demonstrate ROI. In order to do so, you will have had to uncover some important information in the Time Out Call. Things like:

   - What is your weekly traffic count?
   - What is your average sale?
   - What is the profit margin?
   - What is the first-year value of a new customer?
   - What is the lifetime value of a new customer?

Once you have this information, you may be able to demonstrate a reasonable ROI and help reduce the risk in the mind of the potential advertiser. For example, you may be able to show a dentist how you'll only need to generate 10 calls in a month to see a strong ROI on his sedation message.

A word of caution though, don't make the ROI mistake

of trying to calculate on gross. I've witnessed the loss of confidence that comes across a car dealer when the AE says, "All you need to do is sell one car and this $10,000 a month scheduled is paid for!" Not quite! Or the bariatric surgeon who's told, "Hey, at $16,000 a procedure, one new patient covers this $16,000 schedule!" Nope, that's not how it works.

3. **An Incentive.** You can reduce risk in the mind of the prospect by including some sort of incentive. And, just as we ask our clients to have "an astonishing offer" to get better advertising results, our incentives should be "astonishing." The better the incentive, the less risk for the client and the better the chance of a close. The key is to put a strict deadline on the incentive to force your prospect to make a decision.

Reduce risk...

    1)   by including lots of success stories

    2)   by demonstrating reasonable ROI

    3)   by including strong incentives (with a deadline)

...and increase your effectiveness with your clients and prospects.

CHAPTER 45

BALANCE THE NEGATIVE WITH POSITIVE INPUT

ORIGINALLY PUBLISHED: 1/25/2009

2020 Perspective – Seek out positivity! You must. Today, we have greater access to information and opinion than ever, and it can be smothering. The concept of balancing the negative is more important right now than it's ever been. In Bob's words, "...every little thing is gonna be alright!"

There's no question we're all being bombarded with negative stories about layoffs, downturns, bailouts, recessions, etc. Television, radio, newspapers, magazines, the Internet are all loaded with frightening stories of how bad things are and are going to continue to be. It's downright scary!

All the negativity has a pretty dramatic effect on our moods, decision-making, and overall psyche. Maybe you've delayed a major purchase because you're just not sure what the future holds? You are not alone.

I read lots of magazines, particularly when I'm flying. Lately, a 3-hour flight with a heavy dose of *Business Week, Automotive News, Time* and *Inc* is enough to make me want to throw out the white flag and surrender. How much can you read about how bad things are before you just give up?

Well, on my last trip, I happened to grab a copy of *Success* magazine at the airport. Ironically, *Success* bills itself as "What Achievers Read." How refreshing it was to be uplifted by a magazine. It was great brain food—article after article about achieving success in life and controlling one's own destiny. I loved it! It really struck me that I need to balance all the negative I'm exposed to with positive input. It's my decision to either wallow in the negativity or seek uplifting, motivational energy.

I was having lunch with a good friend recently, who's one of those very positive people. This person always has a smile on his face. I was surprised to learn at our lunch that he begins everyday by listening to contemporary praise music. It was just something about him I never knew. He told me it uplifts his spirit and there's no better way for him to start his day.

I suggest that this year, in these conditions, you really need to make a point of seeking out that which gives you a positive boost. Read more uplifting and motivational books and magazines. If you're spiritual, spend more time with what makes you happy. Volunteer your time to help others, be a "go-giver!" Spend more time with successful people and less time with those who bring you down. Eat less of the bad stuff and exercise more. All of these are simple steps to help offset all the negativity with good, healthy, positive input.

CHAPTER 46

BE AN "UNTOUCHABLE"

ORIGINALLY PUBLISHED: 2/14/2009

2020 Perspective – Hey, I think I predicted programmatic buying in this article from 2009! How can you be an untouchable today? I think it's by embracing technology to do your job better. Who will survive this Corona Chaos? The AE who sets up their office to do video meetings. We've already heard of AE's buying green screen backgrounds and investing in lighting. They're running ahead of their peers. Untouchable.

Are you worried about your job security?

In *The World is Flat*, author Thomas Friedman calls them "untouchables." He's referring to people whose jobs cannot be outsourced. Friedman says that in a flat world, you do NOT want to be mediocre. It's really tough out there in our business and if you've had any job security trepidation of late, you need to make yourself an "untouchable."

Friedman describes untouchables as workers who are specialized and really adaptable. What are you doing to make yourself specialized on your sales team? Are you the Internet expert on the staff? Have you created special projects that separate you from the rest of the selling team? Are you the nontraditional revenue expert? These are the revenue-driving specialties that will make you untouchable. And, you have to become really adaptable. You have to constantly upgrade your skills. Friedman says, "Being adaptable in a flat world, knowing how to 'learn how to learn,' will be one of the most important assets any worker can have, because job churn will come faster, because innovation will happen faster."

All this is not meant to scare you. As an Achiever, you're already investing in yourself. However, recently a major broadcast company eliminated almost 10% of its workforce and most of it came from the sales department. In today's environment, nothing is out of the question. Really, this is meant to inspire you, to challenge you to constantly improve, and to make yourself specialized, adaptable—an "Untouchable."

In a recent issue of *Success* magazine, the publisher wrote, "If you want to have more wealth, you have to become more valuable." He says that you can create and maintain only the level of wealth that matches your personal development. If you're not getting better, you can't increase your wealth.

Many of us are facing a year where we may not make as much as we did in previous years. That's always a tough pill to swallow. Once we achieve a certain income level, it's in our minds that we're worth that level and anything less is inappropriate. Guess what, if you have not significantly improved your skills, if you have not become specialized, if you are not adapting, you will not increase your wealth.

Ours is a strange business, where typically we've rewarded those "transactional" sellers more than those who generate the new business. The more veteran the seller, the more transactional our lists become. But transactional is becoming more commoditized. What if some broadcast company decided to place a certain number of avails aside simply for transactional business and created a software program where buyers could go online and order with no need for a salesperson interaction? Doesn't sound that outrageous, does it?

As Daniel Pink wrote in his book, *A Whole New Mind*, "If China or software can do it cheaper, find something else!"

Neither China nor any software will replace specialized marketers who can diagnose a business and create results-oriented advertising strategies. Make yourself an Untouchable in your organization by being special, specialized, and adaptable.

CHAPTER 47

THE TRUTH ABOUT CRABS...

ORIGINALLY PUBLISHED: 2/8/2013

2020 Perspective – I've always loved this story from the first time I heard it. It's so true, especially today! You need to avoid the crabs.

I was riding with a sales manager recently who was very excited about a new hire. He was very high on this new person. After telling me about their work ethic, enthusiasm and drive, he said they'd be a future superstar, **if** he could keep them "away from the crabs."

"Okay," I said, "by 'crabs,' do you mean nasty clients?"

He chuckled and said, "Don't you know about crabs?" Then, he proceeded to tell me the following story...

He said, "When I was a kid, I'd go crabbing with my grandfather. We'd go to the beach and dig up crabs for dinner. After we caught our first crab, my grandfather would have me hold a lid over our bucket so the crab wouldn't climb out. But, as soon as we caught the second crab, the bucket no longer needed a lid. There's a natural occurrence whereby one crab will not allow another to escape. Crabs will latch onto each other and keep pulling escaping crabs back into the bucket. So, as long as you have more than one crab, you don't need a lid."

"I need to keep my new hire away from the crabs. The crabs are the other account executives who'll tell the newbie...

    - why something can't be done

- how bad things are
- what the company needs to be doing differently
- etc., etc., etc.

This is so true! Nothing squashes success more than negative influences that insist on pulling those successful crabs back down in the bucket. Keep your newbies away from those other crabs who can't handle seeing anyone else succeed. Those who will never achieve great success for themselves, and in their own selfish way, will try to keep everyone else around them down as well.

P.S. I had never heard this interesting fact about crabs before, so I Googled "crab story" to see if it was true. Apparently, this is a true fact in nature. Also, many groups have claimed this story and applied it to themselves. From Native Americans to Filipinos to the deaf community, they have all equated the "crab keeping each other down" theory to their own groups. I guess there are crabs in every community and organization. Identify the crabs who may be around you (they typically have claws) and kick them out of your bucket!

CHAPTER 48

5 TIPS TO IMPROVE YOUR LISTENING SKILLS

ORIGINALLY PUBLISHED: 4/20/2008

2020 Perspective – *Whoever asks the questions controls the conversation. But you have to listen as well!*

During the diagnosis call, we spend our time trying to determine client needs through a series of targeted questions. A well-executed "Time Out Call" should reveal the opportunity that's available for you, as an advertising partner, to solve.

We've spent a lot of time focused on the right questions to ask to gain critical information. But, just as important as asking those quality questions is being able to comprehend the answers. Personally, I find the Time Out Call to be the most demanding part of our job. It's an intense 45 minutes that requires not only good questions, but keen listening skills to capture the necessary clues and information. Here are 5 tips to help improve your listening skills.

1. **Have a plan in advance.** One major reason AE's don't listen well is because they're trying to "wing" the Time Out Call. Information is lost as you struggle for the next question, which is attention that should be devoted to listening to answers. I arrive at every Time Out Call with a 6-page "workbook" that helps keep me on track. I have a plan, I'm prepared, I can concentrate on listening to answers without worrying about what comes next.

2. **Take voracious notes.** You have to be listening intently if you're going to correctly capture "soundbites" from the client. Many times, I will verbally repeat a client quote as I'm writing it down in my workbook, to show the client I heard exactly what they said. And, it's very powerful to return with direct quotes attributable to the client in your presentation.

3. **Sit close to the Client.** I find I can concentrate better when I've controlled the surroundings. I choose a seat directly across and as close as possible to the client. I sit on the edge of my seat and lean forward to shorten the distance between the client and me. I want as few distractions as possible between us.

4. **Make lots of eye contact.** When you're concentrating at looking directly at the client—directly into their eyes—you must be attentive, "engaged" as I like to call it. I pick one eye to look directly into and I concentrate on what's being said. I'm sure clients "feel" the intensity in your listening when you do this.

5. **Embrace Silence!** Isn't it amazing that the words "SILENT" and "LISTEN" have the exact same letters? Do not fear silence. It can be your best friend. A silent pause gives the client opportunity to expound on their answer. A silent pause offers you the opportunity to digest the answer. Remain silent and be a better listener!

The biggest compliment paid to me is when I return to see a client, deliver a very detailed Current Situation, and the client says, "Wow! You're a good listener!" It's a critical part of our job. Use these tips to improve your listening skills.

CHAPTER 49

5 THINGS TO BE EXCITED ABOUT IN 2009

ORIGINALLY PUBLISHED: 5/31/2008

2020 Perspective – Budweiser is still no longer owned by an American company!

2008 is finally over! Goodbye and good riddance. In the wake of a year that gave us...
- the biggest economic meltdown since the Great Depression
- record high gas prices
- consumer confidence at an all-time low
- "foreclosures" and "bailouts"

...there is still reason to be excited about the coming new year.

Here are 5 things you should be excited about for 2009:

1. Every advertiser is questioning everything they do right now! Why should you be excited about that? Because there is unprecedented opportunity to approach every advertiser with good ideas and solutions, and they'll be listening. In good years, when all is well with the advertisers' businesses, they're in what we call the "don't rock the boat" mode. There is no reason for them to make changes. Well, now most businesses and advertisers are in fear mode, most of them in a fear mode like they've never been in before. This opens the door for good marketing partners to have greater impact. Be excited that you can approach any potential advertiser and get better attention than you've had in the past.

2. **Health Care.** This category is only getting bigger. In each market we visit, we are seeing more healthcare advertisers having greater success. From bariatric surgeons to sedation dentists to chiropractors to hearing aids, oops, I mean personal hearing devices, the healthcare category continues to grow and yield results for advertisers. Be excited that there is still tremendous untapped potential and at every convention of dentists, doctors and specialists they are discussing marketing principles. Word is out that good marketing is critical to the success of every practice and healthcare facility.

3. **Aging Boomers.** Their 401k's may have taken a hit in 2008, but they still are in control of great wealth and they are aging differently than previous generations, and they watch a lot of television! Focus on categories that enhance the value of their life. Aging in place home improvements, in home health services, financial planning are just a few categories that ring true with the Aging Boomers.

4. **New Rules.** Be excited that the rules of our game are changing. That means that advertising solutions that may have been denied in the past are now open for discussion. Bring those creative sponsorship opportunities to management and see if you can create new partnerships. In December, I met with an advertiser who had been denied weather sponsorships from a station because his :15 bookend strategy didn't fit with the station's news clock. The station slightly re-tooled their clock to accommodate the client for an annual for 2009. Be excited that you can bring new ideas to your station management for consideration.

5. **The Strong will get stronger.** The automotive category is experiencing unprecedented challenges, yet strong dealers are excited that a culling process will occur, and they expect to get even stronger as weaker dealers go away. The same holds true for our business. Weak AE's will not be able to survive and the strong Achievers in our

business can grow and flourish in challenging conditions.

Bonus: Your station website. Most station websites are now delivering tremendous amounts of local traffic. Make 2009 the year you become a multi-platform expert and incorporate the Web into all of your solutions.

While 2008 may have delivered the unthinkable (Budweiser is no longer owned by an American company? That is unthinkable!), 2009 holds plenty to be excited about.

Chapter 50

Don't Lose Alone!

Originally Published: 3/2/2006

2020 Perspective – One of my very favorite lessons from one of my very favorite managers. Now, more than ever, don't lose alone!

Every piece of business is important. Every avail, every sponsorship opportunity, definitely every new client prospect is critical to the continuing success of your department. So, when was the last time you told your sales staff, "Don't lose alone"?

As manager, you are privy to inventory management, overall goals, and special incentives/opportunities that may not be as top of mind with your AE's. You have an overall understanding of the health of the department that any single AE does not. Thus, while it may seem obvious to you, it is a message that needs to be delivered often—"Don't lose alone."

What does "Don't Lose Alone" mean? It means you're in partnership with your sales team. It means sellers *need* to come to you with their struggles and challenging opportunities. Say it often enough and a culture begins to develop that puts you in the mix before it's too late.

From an AE's perspective, they clearly know that you are just as involved as they are, that you take responsibility, along with them, on the challenging accounts. Whether it's due to fear, intimidation or even bravado, it's possible that some AE's may be unwilling to let you know when business is in jeopardy.

If you embrace Don't Lose Alone and open your door, what happens? You'll save some business. You'll strategize more closely with your AE's, maybe make a concession or come up with a great idea that brings you closer to your team. You'll also have the opportunity to stand your ground, decide to walk from some business, and re-affirm boundaries and guidelines where you won't budge. And, your reps will take notice. Don't Lose Alone is the key you give to each of your AE's that allows them access to your office and your help.

You've hired strong professionals and they make good decisions. Don't Lose Alone doesn't undermine their ability to do their job. It simply puts manager and AE firmly on the same ground and it does so before it's too late.

If you haven't lately, share Don't Lose Alone with your AE's in the next sales meeting. Say it often enough, share results, and take greater control of your department and its success.

CHAPTER 51

DONE IS BETTER THAN PERFECT

ORIGINALLY PUBLISHED: 10/14/2009

2020 Perspective – I think this lesson is even more important today! Speed, speed, speed. Don't let yourself get paralyzed by perfection. Get things done!

There's an old business fable that demonstrates the need to do your best always. It goes like this...

An aide to President Roosevelt gave him a speech the aide had been assigned to write. An hour later, President Roosevelt called him to his office, held up the pages of the speech, and asked, "Is this the best you can do?"

The surprised aide hesitated for a moment and said, "Well, sir, there are probably a few points I could make a little clearer."

"Fine," said the President. He handed the speech back to the aide who left the room to rewrite.

A while later, the aide returned and gave his rewrite to the President. After an hour, the President summoned him and asked again, "Is this the best you can do?"

Shocked, the aide replied, "Well, I think so, but let me take another look to see if I can wordsmith it some more."

Once again, the aide left to do another rewrite. A little time passed, and he returned again with his third draft in hand. Once again, Roosevelt asked, "Is this the best you can do?"

This time the aide answered, "Yes sir. This is an excellent speech; one you will feel comfortable delivering."

"Good," said the President. "Now I'll read it."

The moral of the story is that we can usually do any task better. The third version of the speech is what the aide should have turned in the first time.

Imagine if this had happened to you with your manager and one of your important proposals!

It's a great fable with a valuable lesson. However, there are many stories of "missed the boat" opportunities because somebody was faster, not better.

In today's "lightning fast, internet speed, 'get it done yesterday' world," sometimes "done" is better than "perfect."

Sometimes "Ready, Fire, Aim" is the right strategy. Speed in business can be just as critical as anything else. Look at recent business book titles like, *The Age of Speed* and *The Speed of Trust*, and the Bill Gates book, *Business at the Speed of Thought – Succeeding in a Digital World* as proof. Even Six Sigma notes the importance of speed vs. schedule.

When you're preparing those important presentations, it may be appropriate to ask yourself, "Is this the best I can do?" before you hand it to your manager for review. If you have the time, maybe you should take a second and third look at your work before it goes out the door. But be careful, because in today's environment, sometimes "done" is better than "perfect."

Chapter 52

DO YOU SHOW THE PASSION?

ORIGINALLY PUBLISHED: 11/27/2012

2020 Perspective – Over the past few years, I've been discouraged by the lack of passion for our core television product. As our new and amazing digital tools get rolled out, I have sensed less excitement and enthusiasm for our linear, core product. I know that as an AE, you're bombarded each day with clients and prospects who tell you, "Nobody watches TV anymore." I get it. When you hear that over and over, it can mess with your head. Maybe one silver lining in this terribly gray coronavirus cloud will be the resurgence of belief that people still watch a tremendous amount of television, and it's still the most powerful medium ever invented. Go find your passion for it again!

Wow! This past weekend I viewed more of our attorney interviews as we prepare for our satellite conference on 12/12/12 called, "The Big Money Grab – Taking Attorney Money from the Yellow Pages." One interview, in particular, has really stuck with me. It's attorney Tim Misny from Cleveland, OH.

Tim shares many insights on attorney advertising, but one thing he shares is his disappointment in how he's approached by media sellers. In Tim's words, "Only about 5% do it right!" Ouch! That's a pretty scathing indictment of the state of our efforts.

According to Tim, most AE's focus too much on their product and not at all on what they can do for him. I loved his quote. "If an AE says, 'We're number one in six o'clock news,' I say, 'That's great, but what can you do for me?'"

In his most scathing assessment, he equates media sellers with the pumpkin salesperson at his local fruit stand. "I got a $10 pumpkin, a $5 pumpkin, and a $2 pumpkin. Which do you want?"

Tim goes on to say, "You have to convince me that you can help take my business to a whole new level. Persuade me that partnering with you will launch my business to new heights." Tim is a big believer in advertising, particularly television advertising. He credits television advertising with propelling his name, his brand, and his practice to the top of the category in his market.

What really struck me was the passion with which Tim advocates for television. The first time I saw it, I wondered, how many television sellers have that kind of belief in their own product? In fact, Tim says he often advises other business acquaintances to discover the power of television advertising.

I've always believed that buyers of anything want to partner with sellers who are passionately convinced their product is the right choice. Too often, I find myself side-by-side with a media salesperson who doesn't sound convinced themselves that their solution is a great one.

I hope you get a chance to see Tim in our 12/12/12 presentation. You'll witness for yourself his unbridled enthusiasm for advertising, particularly television advertising. In the meantime, ask yourself if you're conveying an unwavering belief that your recommendation can dramatically affect your prospect's business.

CHAPTER 53

5 TIME MANAGEMENT TIPS FROM THE PROS

ORIGINALLY PUBLISHED: 9/2/2008

2020 Perspective – We could all use some reminders on good time management! I wrote this in September of 2008, it was about as close to the bottom as ever. I could see AE's getting distracted and getting off course. Certainly, with the upheaval we're all experiencing right now, we could use these reminders to help put us back on track.

Now that the summer is over, it's a good time to refocus and set your priorities for a successful finish to a very challenging year. I've compiled a few gems and words of wisdom on the topic of time management from a vast collection of wise people...

1. ***"One worthwhile task carried to a successful conclusion is worth half-a-hundred half-finished tasks"*** -Malcolm Forbes

There's plenty on our plate every day. Are you the type who starts a task and then jumps to the next without completing the first? Make it a point to complete item one before moving to item two. You'll enjoy the sense of accomplishment and be more fully productive at day's end.

2. ***"If you want to make good use of your time, you've got to know what's most important and then give it all you've got"*** -Lee Iacocca

Once you set your priorities, be passionate about completing your task.

3. *"Stop and ask yourself, 'Is what I am doing right now, the best thing I could be doing to help me and my career?'"* -Tommy Hopkins

This piece of advice will help keep you on track. If you ask yourself this simple question from time to time (especially those times when you know you may be slacking a bit), you'll guilt yourself back into doing what's most important in your life. Use this self-examination each time you feel that twinge of guilt because you're doing, or considering doing, something that you know is less than productive. This little quote can help keep you out of the coffee shops and away from the commiserating cliques that do nothing to forward your efforts.

4. *"Do the ugliest thing first, everything else will come more easily after that."* -Randy Pausch

If you attack the toughest thing you have to do each day and get it out of the way, you'll have less stress. Try to schedule your toughest (or biggest) appointment of the day early so you avoid a full day of stress and anxiety. If it's painful, get it out of the way early so you can concentrate on being productive.

5. *"If we learn to balance excellence in work with excellence in play, fun, and relaxation, our lives become happier, healthier, and a great deal more creative."* -Ann McGee Cooper

Reward yourself, even for small successes, and celebrate achievement of goals. Promise yourself a reward for completing each task or finishing the total job, and then keep your promise to yourself and indulge in your reward. Doing so will help you maintain the necessary balance in life between work and play.

CHAPTER 54

STAY ACTIVE

ORIGINALLY PUBLISHED: 8/2/2008

2020 Perspective – I originally wrote this in the doldrums of the 2008 Summer. AE's were brow-beaten by now. Months and months of bad news on the economy, uncertainty, confusion, fear. The tendency is to withdraw. As I write this update from my home office, we're under Shelter in Place orders. "Get out there" is not an option right now. But it will be soon. I still believe the answers to your problems are not on your laptop screen. Get out there (when you can) and let opportunity hit you!

Are you finding it tougher and tougher to stay active in your selling efforts these days? The constant stream of bad news—both from our own media reporting to what your clients are telling you on a daily basis—can really take its toll on your attitude. Some days it may seem better to just sit in the office than go out and hear another client or prospect tell you their business is down double digits.

I'm here to tell you that the answer to selling in challenging times is NOT found staring into your computer screen. Activity breeds opportunity, inactivity most certainly does not. I have always loved "The Collision Principle," described in the classic marketing book, *Selling the Invisible*, by Harry Beckwith. Simply, The Collision Principle says that *today, some money is going to exchange hands, it's your job to be in the middle of it.*

"Just get out there, get in opportunity's way, let it hit you," is Beckwith's advice. For all our talk on talent, skill, service, research, etc., sometimes all that matters is who you sat next to in church on Sunday.

So, how can you be more active? Think, eat, and sleep opportunity! Join (or start) a Tip Club. I was a member of a Tip Club for 10 years. It was a collection of twenty-five non-competing businesspeople, who met every Wednesday morning for one hour and shared leads from around our market. A lead was a new business opening, a remodel, expansion, going out of business, etc. We had all kinds of businesses from real estate agents, to interior designers to coffee service. With 25 people bringing at least 2 leads per week, our membership was always in the know as to what was happening around town. That was a better way to spend an hour of my time each week than grabbing a coffee with a crony from another media outlet so we could talk about how terrible things were going.

Increase your attendance at networking events and mixers. I know it's tough after a long day to spend another hour or two talking business, but in today's climate we need to up our efforts. Find those networking events that can expose you to other business decision-makers (as opposed to other media people). Ask your clients if you can join them at their industry and category functions. You'll find more opportunity mingling in a room full of real estate agents or home improvement professionals than you will in a room full of other media salespeople.

Remember, nearly every business is questioning their current advertising practices these days. Increase your profile in your marketplace and engage with those decision-makers who are looking for some guidance. Wear your station logo wherever you go—to the gym, the kids' soccer games, church functions.

As Harry Beckwith writes, Get out there. Almost everywhere. Let opportunity hit you.

CHAPTER 55

THE CLIENT IS HESITANT—A STORY

ORIGINALLY PUBLISHED: 12/18/2007

2020 Perspective – Another example of the power of a good diagnosis

In a recent Achiever's Circle, Jim wrote about what it means when a client hesitates. The scenario is that your 2008 plan is in front of the client and previous years' renewals have been automatic... not so this year. What do you do?

One of Jim's suggestions is to go back and do a full diagnosis call. You may think, "Why do a full diagnosis call? I already know this client inside and out..." Allow me to share a real story with you.

Recently, I was in a market and this exact scenario came up. It was a School of Massage that had partnered with the same TV station for 5 years. The goal is always to fill up the Spring and Fall semesters with students who want a career as a massage therapist. Typically, the client would run a schedule in January and February for the session starting in March. This year, however, the client was hesitating on signing the commitment. The account executive felt he was in jeopardy of losing the business.

I went with the AE to meet the client and do a full diagnosis call. Because I personally had no history with the client, I started from the very beginning and executed a complete diagnosis. I learned that the typical prospects are high school grads and 30-somethings looking for a career change. I learned that the 10-month program costs $7,000. I learned that the competitive landscape had increased dramatically and that this, combined with a struggling economy, presented new challenges to the school.

Then, about a half-hour into our conversation, the client mentioned his "Knead a Friend" program. This, he explained, was his two-day introduction to massage therapy that he would hold two or three weekends each quarter. Then came the game-changer. He told us that about half the people who take the weekend program end up signing on for the full 10-month semester! Bingo! By conducting a complete Time Out Call, we had uncovered the classic "Point of Entry."

We were able to rework the creative from focusing on the full 10-month semester at $7,000, to instead, driving traffic to the two-day, $150 introductory session. We altered the schedule to shorter, more concentrated flights designed to fill up the weekend programs.

The new strategy made sense to the client and we saved the budget.

If we had not gone back and executed a full diagnosis call, we never would have "discovered" the Point of Entry product and probably would have lost the business in 2008.

What should you do when the client hesitates? Don't underestimate the value of a COMPLETE diagnosis call.

CHAPTER 56

THE 3 CHARACTERISTICS YOUR CLIENTS WANT TO INVEST IN

ORIGINALLY PUBLISHED: 12/7/2011

2020 Perspective – More than ever, expertise, integrity, extra-miler!

We think we're selling advertising, or ideas, or solutions, or results. We think our clients are buying time, or exposure, or ratings points, or schedules. But, beyond what we're selling and what we think they're buying, do we really know what our clients/prospects want to *invest* in?

"Invest." That's a much better word than "buy," isn't it? I remember being told by a sales trainer very early in my media sales career to replace the word "buy" with "invest" in my conversations with prospects and clients because "**invest** signals an expectation of a return." It made sense to me back then, it makes sense to me now.

Our clients and prospects don't simply want to buy a schedule or package, they really want to invest—in us, in a partnership. Here are three characteristics your clients want to invest in...

Expertise. Clients want to invest in an expert, not an expert in their business, but in our business. Clients don't expect you to be an expert in their category, knowledgeable, yes, but a full-blown category expert, not really. But they do expect and want to invest in your category expertise. They want to invest with someone who has a proven track record of earning advertising results. And, the more you can demonstrate expertise and ability to do that, the more they'll pay and the longer they'll stay.

Are you doing everything you can to demonstrate your expertise? Are you loaded with success stories of how you have personally helped other businesses earn better advertising results? Are you networked properly and thought of as a media and marketing expert? Do you write and/or speak on the subject regularly? Do you have any special designations or awards? Are you self-promoting your expertise?

Integrity. Clients want to invest in partners who demonstrate integrity. They need to feel that you have their best interest in mind, always. Do anything to the contrary, show any sign of bad judgment, any inkling of unethical, and you've blown your ability to achieve their highest level of trust.

How do you demonstrate integrity? Well, it's really a lifestyle. By definition, integrity isn't forced or fake. As Spike Lee once said, "Do the right thing... always." And, when you make a mistake, fess up quickly, and go above and beyond to make it right. Which brings us to the third characteristic...

Extra Miler. Clients want to invest with partners who will go above and beyond for them, every chance possible. There's great truth to the old saying, "Under promise and over deliver." Do the unexpected for your clients. Surprise them with added value. Mind you, added value doesn't have to mean give away your inventory or other assets. Extra milers simply do things the rest of the pack fail to do. It's holding sales meetings for the client's staff to make sure the campaign is successful. It's networking the client with other strategic partnerships. It's category research and competitive information (gained ethically, see characteristic #2!). I love the line, "There is no traffic on the extra mile." Nothing makes us happier with our purchase/investment than when we get extra mile treatment.

All the salespeople I know, who are achievers—the very

best of the best—are smart, talented professionals and know how to make advertising work. They're all honest, "do the right thing... always" individuals. And, they all go above and beyond for their clients. Anyone would feel privileged to work with them.

CHAPTER 57

FIVE THINGS THAT MAKE ME WINCE!
COMMON PRESENTATION MISTAKES

ORIGINALLY PUBLISHED: 4/26/2009

2020 Perspective – This is the article I wrote in 2009 that was the basis for my first-ever keynote at the NAB Small Market Television Exchange. I guess it went well, as I've been asked back nearly every year since!

I get to share presentation duties with AE's all across the country. There aren't many things that give me greater satisfaction than collaborating with a strong account executive and nailing a great presentation. Conversely, there are some things that happen during presentations that just make me wince.

Here are some presentation mistakes that are all too common...

"We're Number One!" – Ouch! I hear this one all the time. Ask any purchaser of media advertising and they'll tell you their biggest peeve is that everybody claims to be Number One! Folks, even if you are the dominant media outlet in a market, there are better ways to deliver that message than the "We're number one" claim. And, in fact, "we're number one in your demo" alone doesn't help move product. What the client really wants to know is whether you can help them get results with ideas and strategy.

The Page Reader – This is the individual who insists on reading everything on a PowerPoint slide. It's rather

155

insulting to offer a page full of info and feel compelled to read it word for word. The client can do that on their own. Too many AE's insist on cramming in a slide full of info and reading the content verbatim. Less is more here. For a better presentation, put a concept on the page and own the content.

Get your Jarg on! – This is the AE who uses industry jargon with the direct client. Leave that stuff for the media buyer. I have actually witnessed AE's tell local clients things like, "Letterman will do a 2 in November PJ's..." What?!? I can see the store owner thinking, "Did he just tell me Letterman soiled his flannel pajamas?" Please don't use media industry jargon, and that includes any media-created advertising term. You'd be surprised how many potential advertisers have no idea what "bookends" are.

It's not your content – I wince when an AE says, "Here's a success story. It's not my client but..." and proceeds to read bullet points or client quotes with no passion or enthusiasm. You need to "own" the content. Even if the story isn't yours, learn to own the content. Remember, *you* are the presentation. The slide show should only be used as an accompaniment to your talk.

T.M.I. – Too much information! I have watched AE's tout the strength of their six o'clock news, and then NOT INCLUDE IT IN THE SOLUTION! Why even talk about it then? Keep it simple and focused on the next sale. Provide concise and targeted information that supports the strategy. Again, less is more.

"There is a time to say nothing, and a time to say something, but there is never a time to say everything." - Anonymous

CHAPTER 58

WHAT'S YOUR SKIN IN THE GAME?

ORIGINALLY PUBLISHED: 6/6/2009

2020 Perspective – Today, every client you work with wants to feel as though you also have "skin in the game." It's the very definition of advertising "partner." Today, do everything you can to demonstrate skin in the game.

We were deep into the meeting. We had laid out a strong strategy, accompanied by a good creative idea. The client was a Re-Bath franchise. He believed in television, believed in the station, but was still in more "glasses" than he needed to be. We were now asking for 100% of his television budget (which, by the way, amounted to about 90% of his overall budget).

The client was engaged, and all signs were pointing to the fact that he liked what we were presenting. "I'd get rid of my agency," he said. "No need to pay an agency if I'm giving you all my money."

We were okay with that!

Then, the client asked an absolutely brilliant question. "So, what's your skin in the game?"

"What do you mean?" we replied.

He said, "Well, I'm taking all the risk here. You're asking me to put practically all of my money with your station and use your creative idea. What's your skin in the game?"

The station sales manager replied, "Well, if it doesn't deliver the results you're looking for, we lose you as a client! That's our skin in the game."

A fair answer, I thought.

But the client didn't. He said, "That's not enough." He continued, "First of all, you will never completely lose me as a client. I know you're a great station that has worked for me, so I'd be stupid to ax you completely. But if we sit here six months from now and I've given you all of my budget and I haven't seen an increase in results, you get to shrug your shoulders and say 'sorry, let's go back to the original plan.' So, I'm the one who's suffered, not you."

I interjected, "What kind of skin in the game are you looking for?"

"I don't know," said the client. "Just something that makes me feel like you're in this with me."

Let's stop the story here. The client, a very smart business owner and a very astute advertiser, wants to feel like his advertising partners have some skin in the game. Don't all advertisers probably feel that way to some degree? When selling an intangible, we need to realize that buyers walk away from the negotiating table with nothing—no tangible product, no warranty, no guarantee of anything. As the agent in the transaction, we facilitate the buy, and yes, we could make a case that our income, our livelihood, depends on how well we counsel our clients and help them earn results. But, as the client sees it, we, and the station, take their money, run their ads, and hope something good happens. We really have no personal skin in the game.

Now, back to the story....

I said to the client, "If we sat here six months from now and the campaign wasn't producing the results you needed it to, what would have to happen to make you feel we had skin in the game?" (I really didn't have a good answer, so I decided the best thing to do was answer a question with a question— a very reliable technique!)

"I don't know," he said again. "Something that makes me feel like you were in it with me."

"So, if we sat here six months from now and we were consistently under delivering the number of weekly leads and we offered to run an additional bonus schedule on the digital channel, is that something you'd agree to?" I paused.

"Yeah, I'd like to see something like that," the client replied.

Bingo! All he wanted to know is that, as a partner, we'd be willing to offer something as a solution should our strategy under deliver.

Let me make clear that it's not my intention to throw bonus schedules around. I know you value your inventory, and schedules are designed to stand on their own. Instead, the lesson here is to understand how you can make your direct clients feel that you have some "skin in the game." In today's climate, I think it's more important than ever to be proactive in delivering that message.

CHAPTER 59

"You're Fired!" Getting Rid Of Problem Clients

Originally Published: 10/10/2011

2020 Perspective – The very idea of "firing" a client right now seems laughable to you, I get it. But, upon recovery, when this thing is behind us and the arrow starts pointing in the right direction again, use this opportunity to focus on your key clients. During the recovery years after the Great Recession, I knew many AE's who simply told the clients they'd outgrown, "My role at the station has changed moving forward. I have someone else who will be taking over for me and will be handling your account."

Every AE has them: The Problem Child. The Screamer. The Whiner. The Time Sucker. The Late Payer. Some of us have one of each!

Maybe your client never returns your calls. Or, on the flip side, needs to instant-message you at all hours. Their flaws may differ, but the bottom line is the same: They're your worst clients.

These clients are way more work to deal with than the rest of your client list, pay way less or way slower, or all of the above. I always called it the "grief to dollar ratio." Perhaps the best thing you can do is get rid of them.

Why would you do such a thing, especially in this awful economic climate? Difficult clients can sap your energy. It's exhausting, and possibly even annoying, to deal with them.

You dread the days you have to interact with them. Then, you may simply lose the drive to find new business as you run around trying to meet your hell-client's impossible demands.

You may think you need the business, but the reality is as soon as you give a nightmare client the heave-ho, you'll probably find twice as much work elsewhere. The negativity a bad client puts into your life tends to keep you from finding quality clients.

I spent some time with an AE recently who achieved double-digit growth over last year. She was a seasoned veteran with a mature account list. I asked her how she did it. She responded by saying she made the decision to cut the dead weight. She had amassed a very long account list over the years and had trouble letting go of even the smallest clients. Upon realizing that this was holding her back from really growing her best clients and prospects, she "fired" certain accounts. What happened? She had the time to grow those accounts that could really make a difference.

I know what you're thinking right now. "I can't afford to let any client go. They're all important to my overall success." I say to you, "Concentration is the key to all economic success!" Concentrate on those accounts that can deliver the greatest return in 2012 and eliminate those that occupy your efforts for little or no return.

So, you wonder, he's telling me to "fire" a billing account?

Yes, I am. Blow up the slow pay or no pay accounts. Get rid of the little pet accounts that you've handled for years and have outgrown. Give them back to your manager and let him re-assign the account to someone else. Free yourself to dramatically grow those target accounts that are capable of quantum leap increases.

As you put together your 2012 plan right now, can you find 5 billing accounts to turn over to your manager for someone else to handle? Slow pays, no pays, time wasters, dis-respecters, never-going-to-grow accounts that an Achiever should not be dealing with. If you could find 5 of those, and rid yourself of their responsibility, you've just given yourself back the time you need to develop your Key and Target accounts.

How many times this year have you told your clients, "Concentration is the key to all economic success"? Do you really believe that? I hope so, and if it's good enough for your clients, it's good enough for you.

CHAPTER 60

I SNAPPED BACK AT A CLIENT!

ORIGINALLY PUBLISHED: 4/27/2011

2020 Perspective – I'm not very confrontational. I like to be liked. I avoid conflict if I can. But sometimes, you gotta defend yourself! Particularly in today's climate when everyone is on edge.

I was face to face with a client recently and did something I very rarely do, I snapped back!

It takes a lot to get me rattled. I have fallen on my sword so many times I have holes in my belly! I have bitten my tongue so much that I can't even taste things anymore. I don't usually get defensive or snap back... but recently, I did.

It was with Mr. "Don't Rock the Boat," Mr. "I've already got things figured out." During my diagnosis call with him, I almost uncovered one of his little secrets for his business success. Let me be a little clearer. He alluded to something as he answered one of my questions, but wouldn't give me details. I knew I had touched on something important. The client recoiled as soon as he realized he was on the brink of divulging some information he felt was sacred. I'm not talking budget or anything like that—he had a system/process for his business that he felt was the key to his success and he wasn't about to give it away.

When I brought this back up to him during the presentation in my review of our first meeting, he got defensive. I said, "We touched on something in our last meeting, but you were reluctant to share it with me." He acknowledged the "close call."

He then threw out this line, *"And you don't know what you're talking about."*

For some reason, that comment hit me on the chin. I really took great offense to it, probably because this was the presentation meeting—the time when I'm the consultant and I need to shine. We're right in front of an AE and a manager and the client says, "And you don't know what you're talking about!"

Well, I snapped back.

Fortunately, I was standing while I was delivering the presentation, and the client was seated. I walked right over to him, literally leaned over him and said, *"As I shared with you from the very beginning, I am only here to try and help you get better results from your advertising. I can only help using the information that you give me... and I absolutely know what I'm talking about."*

As I mentioned, I normally let a lot of negative comments from clients go. Most of the time I can tell they're just trying to rattle me. My typical defense is to simply press on, unrattled. But this time, I felt it was important to snap back. I guess I felt an attack as direct as "you don't know what you're talking about" couldn't go un-addressed.

In retrospect, I don't think the client was saying I don't know anything about advertising. In fact, I think he was referring to his closely guarded business secret and that I didn't know what I was talking about when referring to that part of our conversation. That's where his comment was coming from, but I took it as a direct slam against my abilities.

So, what happened? Well, it made for a very uncomfortable next couple of minutes, but we proceeded with the presentation. I got right back into presentation mode, regained my composure, and carried on. I actually felt even more confident after I pushed back on the client.

And the client turned into a pussycat! I think even he realized his comment was bold and uncalled for, and after I confronted him on it, he relented.

What's the lesson here? Well, I think we have to pick and choose when we push back. Sometimes falling on our swords, biting our tongues, swallowing our pride is the right approach. I usually execute this approach to confront the outlandish. In other words, when the client does or says something so outlandish it doesn't even warrant a response. The client can't goad you into a fight if you don't push back.

But, a direct attack on you personally, or your medium, and you need to defend yourself. Be firm, be direct, and then move on quickly (I've never seen a good outcome after a really long fight).

CHAPTER 61

GO DEEP, NOT BROAD

ORIGINALLY PUBLISHED: 2/10/2010

2020 Perspective – No matter what the economic climate, going deep as opposed to broad is a smart prospecting tactic.

Tim S. has been an Achiever and part of this group for years. I've had the pleasure of working with him on a number of different occasions and he always brings out the best in me (collaborating with outstanding professionals tends to do that!). Tim does the best job of going deep not broad of any account executive I've ever worked with.

Tim writes a ton of new business. How does he do it? One technique he executes brilliantly is to become a category expert. Tim has determined that it's far better for him to become intimate with a category and exhaust all the potential prospects in his market than it is for him to shotgun his approach to many different categories.

Tim has taken the Doyle principle of "focus" and applied it to his own prospecting efforts!

Are you employing this approach? Should you gain expertise in relevant categories and then penetrate deep into those categories, instead of shotgunning your prospecting approach?

When you think about all the opportunity out there, it is tempting to keep all your options open. After all, the more potential customers you have, the more sales you'll get, right?

Not so fast. Some might say the exact opposite is true. Some might say that by narrowing your targets, you'll increase your effectiveness. Selling may still be "a numbers game" but maybe the gameboard has changed. It may no longer be about spending hours on the phone, calling hundreds of different prospects, hoping to find someone who will meet with you. Selling today is about targeting the types of businesses where you'll have a high likelihood of success. It's about limiting the number and types of prospects that best fit your pre-established parameters and digging deep in the category.

Here are 5 tips to going deep, not broad:

1. Pick categories in which you may have existing expertise or passion. If you can show some unique reason that demonstrates you have special expertise, exploit it! I once worked with an AE who sold furniture in a previous career. She "spoke the language" and understood the category better than most other AE's. She did very well with furniture stores.

2. Find a category VBR. Bed bugs are back in a big way. That's a VBR (Valid Business Reason) to dig deep in the pest control category to find the smart marketer who wants to own the Bed Bug Expert position.

3. Find *enabling conditions*. Enabling conditions exist when timing is ripe for your solution to solve a problem your prospects are, or will be, facing. I once worked in a state that announced a huge tax increase on cigarettes. One smart AE called on every "smoking cessation solution" (hypnosis, laser therapy, etc.) available.

4. Pick categories where you can demonstrate a track record of success. Be careful, though, as many businesses don't want to hear how successful you've made their direct competitor. Instead, demonstrate success in "like categories." For example, tell the chiropractor about the success you created with a pain clinic. Tell the kitchen remodeler about the success you earned for a window replacement company.

5. Create a product that is category specific. Create a Women's Health segment in your noon news that's supported on your website. Develop an "All in a Day's Drive" feature that focuses on local events and destinations. Increase your prospecting success by having a pre-existing product to stimulate interest.

Jill Konrath puts it this way: Your Expertise + Your Offering = Business Improvement

CHAPTER 62

CONTROL PRODUCTION, CONTROL THE ACCOUNT

ORIGINALLY PUBLISHED: 3/30/2008

2020 Perspective – While I still believe it's critical to be involved in the creative process, I think the 2020 update might be, "control digital, control the account." The closest relationships I see today are happening with the intimacy of our digital tools. That said, in the upheaval of the current climate, creative discussions are paramount, and you need to be part of them!

Here's a belief I have: Whoever controls production, controls the account.

I'm convinced that the media rep who helps the client get their creative produced and distributed, is the media rep that has the greatest control over the success of the advertising.

So, it always bothers me when account executives are willing to "let the cable guys do it, 'cause they'll do it for free" or "let him go to a production house because they have better equipment." To truly partner with an account, to really have their best interest in mind and want to grow with them, you should strive to control the client's production. Let's explore the benefits...

I think the biggest benefit of controlling production is in the amount of face time with the client during critical decision-making times! We've all seen great ideas get twisted and turned in the creative process. When you control production, you're involved (or should be) in the critical decision-making process. Your client needs you to guide the process through to the end result, agreed upon during the presentation process. You don't want to give up that responsibility to anyone else, especially a competitor.

Don't confuse your *relationship face time* with *decision-making face time*. Here's what I mean... relationship face time is all the meetings, lunches, client trips, etc., that help build the personal relationship you grow with your client. It's all well and good, and critical to the overall health of your working relationship. However, you can have the best personal relationship with a client, be the "favorite AE" in the market, but you severely jeopardize your ability to help the client earn results if you're not in on the hardcore decision-making processes—one of the most important of which is production.

Controlling production also moves you away from those conversations we don't want to have—ratings, cost per point, etc.—and closer to the conversations we do want to have, such as specific needs and results. When you're the rep in the market who controls the client's production, you're a little more insulated from things like the occasional bad ratings book.

One more note: even if the other guys offer free production, almost all clients know there's nothing "free" in life. They know, or believe, they're paying for it somehow. There's a perceived value with "free." To wrestle a client away from the other guy's "free" production, you need to create greater value with your service. The quickest way to create that value is with great ideas and success stories.

Controlling the production isn't a little more work, it's a LOT MORE work. But it's worth it. It can, and should, lead to a closer partnership, which should also translate to bigger budgets.

Chapter 63

"Every Day In The Duck Woods Is Different"

Originally Published: 3/29/2009

2020 Perspective – There are so many great characters out there, and whether times are booming, or times are busting, they need our help. Yet, I learn just as much from them as they do from me.

One of the best parts of my job is that I get to travel all over the country and meet with really interesting, and many times brilliant, businesspeople. Over the years, I've met a number of colorful characters, from Phil the one-eyed septic expert in Upstate New York, to Dr. Johnny G., the weightlifting eye surgeon in Middle Georgia. Through my hours of interviews, I get to collect some pretty interesting quotes. Here are 3 of my favorites from recent client Time Out Calls...

1. From Gerry, the Replacement Windows business owner in Arkansas:

"Every day in the duck woods is different." We were discussing why it was important for Gerry to be active with his advertising 12 months a year. Gerry was telling me that he likes to be on TV on a consistent basis because, "every day in the duck woods is different." Meaning, that each day a new crop of prospects comes into the sales cycle and he wants to be in front of them when they're ready. He realizes he's advertising to a passing parade and there will be a new

parade coming by tomorrow who never saw his ad today, so he has to be in front of them with his message.

2. From Auggie, the owner of The Good Feet Store in Pittsburgh:

"I am in the media business selling arch supports." Auggie realizes that he always needs to be advertising to drive new prospects. His is a one-time sale, so he constantly needs to fill the funnel. In Auggie's mind, he's really in the advertising business. His product—arch supports—is simply the widget he sells.

3. From Anthony, the General Manager at the Hyundai dealership in Knoxville:

"Like I tell my salespeople all the time, the three most important words in selling are, 'you told me.'" Anthony was impressed with the Current Situation page in our proposal. We had used direct quotes from the Time Out Call and he kept nodding each time I used the phrase, "You told me." When we were all done with the presentation, he made it a point to compliment me on this technique. He said, "Like I tell me salespeople all the time, the three most important words in selling are 'you told me.'"

CHAPTER 64

SOMETIMES YOU NEED TO CHECK YOUR EGO... OR... A HOT IDEA MELTS A COLD OBJECTION EVERY TIME!

ORIGINALLY PUBLISHED: 3/18/2008

2020 Perspective – In the months to come, clients and prospects will be short, impatient, and maybe, downright rude. Understand the pressure our advertising decision-makers are under in these awful conditions. You want them to spend money on advertising, they're sweating payroll. Check your ego. Bring ideas. Now, more than ever!

I had one of those calls recently that was loaded with sales lessons. So much was going on that I have to give this article two titles!

I had met with a business that was an "alternative" to payday loans. This was a guy who "wasn't like those other guys who just want to take advantage of people." He insisted his product was different in that he actually helped restore bad credit.

Lesson number one: **Sometimes you just have to check your ego.**

This guy was a typical driver, as many entrepreneurs are. He felt it important in the Time Out Call to let me know he was an engineer and had worked for many big companies. I'm totally okay with people who are proud of their accomplishments. It was during my return visit that things got uncomfortable.

We sat for our presentation and he immediately told me he was short on time. I assured him I'd move along quickly. Upon taking him through the Current Situation, he interrupted, saying he didn't need me to read to him. He told me that he's given presentations to "the board at GM" and would never insult the client by reading to them. An attempt to defend myself was futile, so I suggested we move on.

His impatience was obvious with every page. Finally, I decided to just skip to the Recommended Strategy. Here's where things really fell apart. After I delivered my first strategic suggestion, he goes off on how I completely missed the boat. He said I didn't listen to his answers in the Time Out Call. (Ouch! That really hurt!) According to the client, I was totally incorrect in my diagnosis and recommended strategy.

I have never folded up the tent poles and given up, but this time, I was really close. I was seriously considering ending the call, about to say I wouldn't waste his time or mine by continuing. Based on his negative reaction to everything I'd presented, I would have been justified.

I also considered getting into a heated debate with him. I did try to defend everything he was questioning, but he was having none of it. So, I sat on my ego. Rather than try to prove I was right, I decided not to fight with the client. Sometimes, you just have to check your ego.

In a last-ditch effort, and because I had done the work, I suggested we go right to the creative idea. The client reluctantly agreed.

Lesson number two: **A Hot Idea Melts A Cold Objection Every Time!**

I went directly to the creative concept I had put together for him. I put my best announcer's voice on and read him the script I had written.

Bingo! He loved it! He asked how soon we could get it produced and created a budget for the following month (he had not been on the air in a year!).

Had I let my ego get the best of me, I would have gone to battle with this driver or called it quits and walked away (calling him all kinds of nasty names under my breath). Instead, I put my ego aside and just kept plodding along in the call.

And, without a good, complete piece of creative, this meeting would probably have been the last between client and station. It's amazing that no matter how badly the rest of the presentation goes, if you have a really good idea, clients will react.

The idea will work, and the client will continue to be very difficult to work with, but he'll continue to spend.

Sometimes to be successful, we have to check our egos. And, a hot idea melts a cold objection every time.

CHAPTER 65

LET THE CLIENT TELL THEIR STORY

ORIGINALLY PUBLISHED: 3/14/2009

2020 Perspective – Your clients and prospects have never been more "sick." Let them tell you their story (if they want to).

"Unfortunately, medicine sees anecdote as the lowest form of science." -Dr. Jack Coulehan

You're in the room and the doctor walks in.

"What seems to be the problem?" he asks.

"Well, I was lifting weights, which I do about three times a week. Well, really probably just twice a week. I try and mix in some cardio. Anyway, I was doing curls, it was my upper body day..."

"Look, just give me the facts," interrupts the doctor.

Wait a minute. I am giving the facts. I'm just trying to be complete. Imagine if your doctor interrupted you or seemed uninterested in hearing your full story when he was doing his diagnosis. From your perspective, every bit of information you share is important as you tell your story.

When we do a Time Out Call with clients, the same holds true.

Clients love to talk about their business. It's our job to let them. Sure, we need to uncover the facts—their core customer profile, the competitive landscape, their budget and spending habits—but we also gain extremely valuable information that's wrapped in the stories they tell.

Many times, I'm pressed for time and would like to cut

off a long-winded client. However, I have found that the more I let a client tell their story, the more information I get, and just as importantly, the more comfortable the client feels with me.

Today, when most businesses are "sick," it's more important than ever that we let them tell their stories. As physician Dr. Howard Brody says, "Stories—that's how people make sense of what's happening to them when they get sick. They tell stories about themselves. Our ability as doctors to treat and heal is bound up in our ability to accurately perceive a patient's story."

In fact, many med schools are now teaching classes in Narrative Medicine, where they teach the ability to listen more empathetically to the stories the patients tell and to "read" those stories with greater understanding. "Tell me where it hurts" becomes "Tell me about your life."

As "marketing doctors," we need to take that same approach with our clients. Oftentimes, one of my closing Time Out Call questions is, "Tell me a story about a satisfied customer." I want to know about the last Thank You note they received from a raving fan. What was it that went so well, what motivated someone to share their thoughts? That's good stuff to know, and it makes great creative fodder.

CHAPTER 66

OWN THE MATERIAL

ORIGINALLY PUBLISHED: 1/17/2009

2020 Perspective – I wrote this article at the beginning of 2009, when every opportunity to present mattered and it was imperative to bring your "A" game to each meeting. It's like that today. You cannot afford a "mulligan" on any call, especially a presentation. Own the material!

The presentation was in full swing. Things were moving along quite well—the client was engaged, and the AE was doing a fine job presenting. And then, thud!

We got to the local success stories portion of the presentation. The AE stumbled and bumbled their way through 3 slides—slides that should have been the most powerful part of the presentation. What went wrong? The AE didn't own the material. The success stories were someone else's and the AE couldn't effectively deliver the message.

How many times have you grabbed some one-sheets out of the rack or used presentation pages or slides that someone else created and you really didn't own the material? The client can see right through this.

When you don't own the material, here's what happens...
- You stumble your way through the page because you're not 100% sure what the intent of the page is
- You lose control because you become derailed
- You turn off the client because you look less professional
- You turn off the client because you're wasting their time

(if you included a page but aren't deliberate in presenting it, you're wasting the client's time)

- You're missing an opportunity to make an effective point

It's certainly okay to use one-sheets or slides that were created by someone else, but you need to make sure you have rehearsed how you're going to present the slide and, most importantly, know why it's included in your presentation. I think many times AE's include pages in their proposals just to fill up space. Then, when it comes time to present certain slides, they drop the ball.

Let's get back to the specific example I used to start this article. Success stories from your station are probably the single most critical element to reduce risk and bring you closer to a sale. I hope you're all aggressively collecting stories earned by your station to include in your proposals. Everyone on your sales team should be sharing these. Take the time to learn the details of the story so you can share it effectively. Even if you had nothing to do with the story, you should be able to deliver it with sincere enthusiasm and pride in your station's ability to help advertisers succeed.

I deliver national success stories during my presentations, most of which I had nothing to do with! But I deliver them with enthusiasm and pride, as being wonderful examples of businesses that adopted our principles and have seen great success. The clients to whom I'm presenting never need to know that I personally had nothing to do with the creation of the story. And, I've sometimes contacted the station and AE who was responsible for a success story, so I can fully understand all the details and own the material.

Before you include any page or slide in your presentation, make sure you own the material!

CHAPTER 67

MY MOM ALWAYS SAID, "BE ON YOUR BEST BEHAVIOR"

ORIGINALLY PUBLISHED: 12/7/2010

2020 Perspective – If you're not offering to host the presentation, you're making a mistake! It's called "home field advantage" for a reason. Get your client or prospect to come into your environment for the presentation. Treat them like the cherished guest they are. Introduce them to talent, support staff, managers, and production, and make them feel like they're part of the family. We've had plenty of AE's tell us that the clients or prospects will never come to the station facility. "We're not convenient" or "they don't have the time" are the excuses we hear. Then, we ask and the client doesn't hesitate to accept. And our closing percentage goes up.

As a kid, anytime we were in the car on the way to someone's house for a visit, my Mom would always say, "Now kids, I need you to be on your best behavior!" We knew the things we might get away with at home were NOT allowed when we were guests at someone else's place. No horseplay, no rough housing, no tantrums, no bad language, no outbursts, none of that was allowed as a guest in someone else's home.

Apparently, my mom is not the only parent who drilled "be on your best behavior" when you're a guest. Allow me to explain...

Recently, I was in a market to do Time Out Calls and ended up in the office of a marketing director for a large healthcare system. The client was an unruly tiger! He challenged my every question, fought back, and was all around non-cooperative. He got up and left the room without explanation at one point in the meeting, and he seemed more interested in his soda than our conversation. I asked my magic wand question, "If I could wave a magic wand and accomplish one thing with your advertising, what would that one thing have to be?" He looked at me and said, "I don't know, try and WOW me..."

I left the meeting feeling frustrated and ineffective.

As has been our process in recent years, we always invite the client to the TV station for the presentation. A few weeks after our first meeting, I was back in town to do presentations. I saw the unruly healthcare client on the list and was not looking forward to that meeting.

Later in the week, the meeting time came. I took a deep breath and prepared for battle. When the client arrived, he was a completely different individual. He was polite, courteous, engaged, and very pleasant. This tiger had turned into a pussy cat!

I think he knew, as a guest in the TV station, he had to be on his best behavior! Nothing else had changed in the situation, he simply acted differently when taken out of his own element.

Hosting presentations at your office is a powerful way to increase your chances of a positive outcome. Do as much as you can to stack the deck in your favor, a tablecloth-covered treat table with cookies or sweets, fresh hot coffee, tea, and cold sodas on display, a free mug to take away. Do whatever you can to make your prospect feel like a cherished "guest" of yours and they will be on their best behavior.

CHAPTER 68

YOUR PERSONAL "FEEL GOOD" FOLDER

ORIGINALLY PUBLISHED: 1/28/2010

2020 Perspective – *The shortest article I've ever written. Two sentences! I learned of this idea from a superstar account executive who always had a terrific attitude. My 2020 update: keep two folders—a hard copy and an Outlook folder. You're good at what you do. Your job is important. You help business grow and thrive. Take time to remind yourself of the great work you do!*

Keep a folder in your file cabinet filled with "attaboys/attagirls," thank you notes, and any other accomplishments or recognition. Refer to it from time to time to make yourself feel good.

CHAPTER 69

ARE YOU A GOOD SOLDIER?

ORIGINALLY PUBLISHED: 11/20/2008

2020 Perspective – I'm choosing this as my last article. I think it's my favorite of all the articles I've ever written. In these new "worst I've ever seen" conditions, I believe it to be truer than ever. We need good soldiers in this business. Watch what you say, watch what you do, lead by example, especially if you're a veteran. Our newbies need our support and guidance more than ever before. If you've survived the other "worst I've ever seen" watershed moments, you at least know that "this too shall pass." Those who have come on board post Great Recession have never experienced adversity like this. As you struggle to keep your head above water, be sure to lend support to your peers.

Time for a little gut check. In these, the most tumultuous times in our careers, are you being a good soldier?

A good soldier is someone who consistently displays the right attitude, no matter the conditions. A good soldier supports his/her leadership. A good soldier does whatever he/she can do to help the entire platoon. A good soldier volunteers for the tough missions.

The reason I write this is because you're probably a leader on your sales team. Achiever's Circle members typically are. And, as a team leader, you have certain responsibilities to uphold—the Good Soldier responsibilities. I'm reminding you about this because we're in the types of conditions that can cloud your understanding. So BE CAREFUL. Watch what you say, be careful of your actions.

Let me share a story. Years ago, I was on the sales staff of a radio station. I had some seniority and was a top biller. At a typical b*tch lunch (you know, where all the sellers go to lunch together to complain about how crappy things are), one newer team member made a comment about how tough things were. I said, in a very unflattering way, "I know, I've seen your billing!"

Truth is, I hadn't seen his billing, I was just making a stupid, cocky comment. I had no idea if he was having a lousy month or a great month. I was just being a jerk.

Years later, that newbie became my manager. One day, he reminded me of the comment I'd made about his billing. He told me that my comment devastated him for about a week. To be honest, I barely remembered making the comment. But here was his lesson for me. He said, "Tom, you don't even realize what kind of weight your comments carry around here. You're a leader in these halls. People watch what you do and say more than you realize. So, when you make little jokes or negative comments of any kind, people listen." He said, "I need you to be a good soldier. I need you to support my decisions, respect corporate, and be a positive force in these halls."

I was blown away. Until he pointed this stuff out, I really wasn't aware of it. I just thought that anyone who would listen to anything I said was nuts to begin with! But, of course, his advice for me was spot on. From that point forward, I've monitored my words and actions to make sure I'm being a good soldier.

So, I ask you, are you being a good soldier? You probably carry more weight on your team than you realize. Others are likely taking notice of your attitude and actions in these conditions more than you realize.

Here are 10 good soldier specifics you can do:

- Get your paperwork in on time, always
- Refrain from sarcasm or negativity, even if you're only joking
- Sell the stuff that needs to be sold (Internet, sports packages, etc.)
- Create some proposal research that everyone can use
- Offer to lead a sales meeting
- Share your success stories
- Show up early
- Avoid the corporate b*tch sessions
- Buy something nice for the whole office to enjoy
- Help a newbie (they may become your manager one day!)

CONCLUSION

April 6, 2020

I came up with the idea to assemble this collection a week ago. I wanted to produce something to offer support and encouragement to all the media account executives and managers who are battling the toughest war they've ever been in. My attitude toward our future is better today than it was a week ago. Revisiting these stories has reminded me that even in the worst of times, we play an important role in the health of our local businesses. We also need to help our coworkers navigate dark waters.

I'm not sure how long the darkness will last. I do know that the next few months, maybe years, won't be easy. I also know that it won't last forever.

I think this crisis will leave it's mark more deeply than any other. Business models will change. I'd encourage every manager, every company, to re-think traditional office hours. I challenge AE's to prove you can be effective without having to show up to the office every morning and every afternoon. In the few weeks of this crisis, I've seen the best of us pick up our game. I've seen home studios assembled for virtual meetings and social media posts that were informative and useful. I've seen companies, stations, managers, and AE's find creative ways to support their advertisers. It's uplifting. Thank you for all you do.

I do believe this. Your best work, your career-defining

moment, is just ahead. I know my greatest success stories of helping local advertisers came from the darkest days of the recession.

In August of 2009, I met with Michelle Laws, owner of Laws Abbey Flooring in Jonesboro, Arkansas. She owned a struggling carpet store in the midst of the worst economic conditions we'd ever seen. She was trying different media, different messages, and nothing was working for her. As I pressed her for a differentiator, she casually mentioned, "Well, we do have a pretty good guarantee." With minimal expectations I said, "Okay Michelle, what's your guarantee?"

She said, "If we install your hardwood floors, you've got sixty days to decide whether you like them. If within sixty days, you decide you don't like your new hardwood floors, I'll come back, rip them out, and replace them. Free. Installation included."

Wow. Astonishing.

We made her, Laws Abbey Flooring, Home of the Sixty Day Walk On It Warranty.

She began her campaign in October 2009 and she had the biggest October in her company's 19-year history. She continued the campaign and was up double-digits in 2010. Nobody was up double-digits in 2010.

About seven years later, Laws Abbey Flooring Center in Jonesboro, AR moved into their new location, twice the square footage of their old store.

I did my best work in the darkest times.

Go create your career-defining success.

Be safe. Stay healthy. Wash your hands. I'll see you soon.

Tom Ray

ABOUT THE AUTHOR

Tom Ray is Executive Vice President of Jim Doyle & Associates. He has over 30 years of LOCAL media experience. From radio, to broadcast and cable television, to digital development and marketing, Tom's diverse background gives him a unique perspective on driving results for the LOCAL advertiser.

For more than a decade, he has travelled the country, helping businesses discover what works and what doesn't in local advertising.

Tom is a member of the National Speakers Association and has achieved their highest designation of Certified Speaking Professional (CSP). He has been a featured speaker for the National Association of Broadcasters, at various State Broadcasters Association events, and has shared his advertising insights for thousands of local businesses in markets big and small across the US.

Also by Tom Ray: *Branding is OUT, Results are IN! Lessons for the LOCAL Advertiser*

Made in the USA
Las Vegas, NV
03 December 2020